FAMILY INTERVENTION
WITH PSYCHIATRIC PATIENTS

FAMILY INTERVENTION WITH PSYCHIATRIC PATIENTS

Edited by

Raymond F. Luber, M.Div.

Fayette Community Mental Health Center
Uniontown, Pa.

Carol M. Anderson, Ph.D.

University of Pittsburgh
Pittsburgh, Pa.

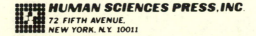 **HUMAN SCIENCES PRESS, INC.**
72 FIFTH AVENUE,
NEW YORK, N.Y. 10011

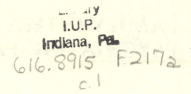
Printed in the United States of America
23456789 987654321

Library of Congress Cataloging in Publication Data
Main entry under title:

Family intervention with psychiatric patients.

    Includes index.
    1. Family psychotherapy.   I. Luber, Raymond F.   II. Anderson,
Carol M., 1939-.   [DNLM: 1. Family therapy.   WM 430.5.F2   [241p]
RC488.5.F325   616. '89 '156   82-3020
ISBN 0-89885-031-2   AACR2

CONTENTS

PREFACE

Family intervention with psychiatric patients has received considerable clinical and scholarly attention in recent years. Increasingly, one
hears professionals of various disciplines saying that they are doing
"family therapy" or wish to become "family therapists." This
declaration, however, communicates a variety of messages depending
upon the conceptualizations held by the speaker and listener. Currently, there is no single, commonly accepted definition of "family
therapy." On the contrary, several distinct approaches to the
treatment of psychiatric problems and the proliferation of treatment
somewhat confusing picture for the clinician as well as the scholar.

At the same time, research findings and clinical experience seem
to indicate that both the etiology and treatment of psychiatric
disturbances involve more than simply the intrapsychic problems of
the so-called "identified patient." Indeed, more and more we are
seeing an emphasis placed on the family system as a locus of investigation and treatment in the psychiatric arena. It is rare to find a psychiatric facility or a therapist working in such a setting who does not
give at least verbal support to the involvement of the family in the
treatment process.

The convergence of these two developments, namely, the increased emphasis on the role of the family in the etiology and
treatment of psychiatry problems and the proliferation of treatment
approaches, has posed significant difficulties in the field. These difficulties involve, mainly, the adaptation of treatment approaches to a
new and somewhat unique setting, the psychiatric hospital or clinic.
Generally, theories of family intervention have been developed and
implemented with non-psychiatric populations. One possible excep-
tion, the Bowen Theory, although initially developed for the
treatment of families of schizophrenics, has since been utilized with a
totally different population and currently is not considered to be
applicable to psychiatric situations by many of its spokesmen and
practitioners.

This volume is intended as a preliminary attempt to fill this gap
between theory and practice. It is our hope that both clinicians and
theorists will become acquainted with ideas and techniques useful in
the treatment of the psychiatric population and in the continued investigation of the most efficacious methods of involving the family in

6 FAMILY INTERVENTION WITH PSYCHIATRIC PATIENTS

this particular setting. We consider this book to be an initial statement, not the final word, and look forward to the continued development of thought in this area.

Many individuals need to be recognized for their contributions to this volume. The various authors, of course, deserve special thanks for their efforts in applying the specific treatment approaches to a situation which, for many, was a rather unique and somewhat uncharted territory. Our appreciation is also expressed to Norma Fox of Human Sciences Press for her patience in a situation which extended over a far longer period than was initially anticipated. Finally, we wish to express our gratitude to Gretchen MacDonell and Selma Stone for their indispensible secretarial support.

Raymond F. Luber
Carol M. Anderson

LIST OF CONTRIBUTORS

Carol M. Anderson, Ph.D.
Associate Professor of Clinical Psychiatry
Department of Psychiatry
University of Pittsburgh

Susan Schilling Erstling, M.S.W.
Assistant Professor of Clinical Psychiatry
Department of Psychiatry
University of Pittsburgh

Suzanne Goren, R.N., Ph.D.
Formerly Director, Intramural Program
Philadelphia Child Guidance Clinic

Bernard G. Guerney, Jr., Ph.D.
The Pennsylvania State University

Louise F. Guerney, Ph.D.
The Pennsylvania State University

Raymond F. Luber, M.Div.
Executive Director
Fayette Community Mental Health Center

Morton D. Schumann, M.S.W.
Associate Professor
Department of Psychiatry
Medical College of Virginia

Michael A. Solomon, D.S.W.
Associate Professor of Psychiatry
University of Colorado

Edward Vogelsong, Ph.D.
Institute for the Development of Emotional
and Life Skills, Inc.

Eugenie G. Wheeler, M.S.W.
Private Practice
Ventura, California

DEDICATION

This volume is dedicated to family members (both nuclear and extended) and significant others who, knowing that "down the ancient corridors and through the gates of time, run the ghosts of days (and dreams) that we left behind" (Fogelberg, 1981), nevertheless, work to "differentiate a self" despite the specters.

Raymond F. Luber

Chapter 1

INTRODUCTION AND OVERVIEW

Raymond F. Luber

Introduction

In recent years, the importance of family intervention in the treatment of psychiatric patients has received increased attention. This has been evident in a number of ways. For example, one survey of the field reported that "it seems to be an almost universal feeling among respondents that family therapy is more effective and that results can be seen more quickly and often more clearly" than with other treatment methods (Group for the Advancement of Psychiatry, 1970). In another area, the literature presenting reasons for, and methods of, treating families has steadily increased. Indeed, one recent review states that "more than twice as many items referring to family therapy, couples therapy, and marital therapy and counseling were identified in the 1977 literature than in the previous year" (Lubin, Reddy, Taylor and Lubin, 1978, p. 530). And, finally, although empirical investigations of this treatment form are still limited, it is evident that increased research emphasis is being placed on this crucial aspect of psychiatric treatment (DeWitt, 1978; Wells and Dezen, 1978).

In general, this increased emphasis on the family has resulted from a growing conviction that the identified patient, that is, the individual whose "symptoms" precipitated the initiation of treatment, does not exist in a vacuum nor are the effects of the treatment limited to the patient. For example, Maxmen, Tucker and LeBow (1974) state that "the most important reason for involving the family is to sustain and enhance the patient's rehabilitation post discharge" (p. 197). And, as Rabiner, Molinski and Gralnick (1962) put it: "It is clear that changes in the primary patient, along with decisions one makes for him or helps him to make for himself, impinge upon the family group with effects one must take into account" (p. 619). Given these basic assumptions, it is understandable that increased attention has been given to family intervention in the treatment of psychiatric patients.

With this increased emphasis, however, has come a proliferation of treatment approaches to the family (Guerney, 1977; Mash, Hamerlynck and Handy, 1976; Minuchin, 1974; Skynner, 1976). The treatment principles articulated in these approaches have been widely adopted by clinicians working in the psychiatric setting, including those primarily treating an inpatient population. There are two important issues that must be addressed in this attempted application. The first issue involves empirical support for family intervention with psychiatric patients. The second issue concerns problems which appear to be unique to the psychiatric setting and may have significant implications for the application of family treatment principles to this population.

In regard to empirical support for the various approaches to family therapy, several comprehensive reviews have appeared which carefully deliniate current research status (DeWitt 1978; Gurman and Rice, 1975; Gurman and Kniskern, 1978; Luber, 1978; Wells and Dezen, 1978). In general, these reviews have concluded that many questions are as yet unanswered regarding the efficacy of family therapy; indeed, at this point there is a dearth of outcome studies related to family therapy with psychiatric patients (especially hospitalized patients). In addition, there seems to be some contradictory evidence regarding the utility of family therapy with adult schizophrenic patients (Guttman, 1973; Gould and Glick, 1976; Lee and Mayerson, 1973). Finally, many studies suffer from serious methodological problems which detract from their value. One of these problems, similar to that encountered in group therapy research (Parloff and Dies, 1977), has been the failure to carefully describe the components of the particular treatment approach being used, making replication a difficult problem. Thus, the situation at the present time seems to be that although family therapy has greatly expanded its theoretical and conceptual parameters, hard empirical evidence still does not exist to carefully prescribe the treatment technique, especially in the psychiatric setting.

A second problem related to the application of family therapy approaches to the psychiatric patient is the growing recognition that certain factors unique to the setting may have serious implications which make extensive revisions in theoretical orientation necessary. These factors, although accentuated in the inpatient setting, seem to be applicable to all psychiatric patients and are encountered in varying degrees in different settings.

This chapter will highlight several of these problems briefly. They will be discussed in greater detail by the various contributors to this volume as they individually describe the application of their particular approach to the treatment of families in the psychiatric setting. In addition, possible alterations or revisions in theory necessitated by the treatment setting, techniques most applicable to the setting, and specific methods of approaching problems dictated by the theoretical position, will be considered by each contributor.

Overview of Problem Areas

Stigma associated with the hospital setting. It has long been recognized that there is a social stigma associated with both psychiatric patients and psychiatric hospitals. Rabkin (1974) points this out clearly when she states that "mental patients have for years been regarded with more distaste and less sympathy than virtually any other disabled group in our society" (p. 10).

Mrs. L is a 35-year-old mother of two who was being treated in partial hospitalization. This hospitalization was the culmination of a series of significant events occurring over a five-year period which precipitated symptoms of anxiety and depression. The events included the death of her father, her own divorce, establishing a relationship with another male by whom she became pregnant, a subsequent abortion, the death of her mother in a hit-and-run automobile accident, and her remarriage. Family treatment was to be initiated to consider several issues including Mr. L's role in the raising of his stepchildren, Mrs. L's continued concerns about her identity and self esteem and the adjustment problems facing Mrs. L's children. After one session, the husband refused to return to the hospital *after saying* that he did not want to be seen entering a psychiatric facility, that being in the building made him uneasy and that he was fearful some physical harm might come to the children because of the types of patients treated in the setting. He stated that he was willing to participate in family sessions but only in another setting. Consequently, several meetings were conducted in the family home.

Despite some positive changes in public attitudes in recent years, resulting largely from more accurate information about mental illness, psychiatric hospitals generate a great amount of stigma and fear (Welch, 1979). It is safe to say that much of this stigma is still rooted in persistent stereotypes. Anderson (1977) points out that these stereotypic views can have a direct effect on family involvement in the treatment process, an effect which is generally negative and often expressed in the form of resistance to involvement.

Another serious effect of this stigma and fear can be that families delay seeking help until a crisis situation develops. At this point, treatment efforts must be directed toward resolution of the immediate crisis, reserving more comprehensive family issues until a later time. Although times of crisis can, indeed, serve as propitious opportunities for making changes in family relationships and structures, they may also solidify existing negative patterns. Delay in treatment, consequently, is not a universally advantageous situation.

Thus, in the psychiatric setting one of the initial questions facing the family therapist is: ''How do you involve the family in the treatment process?'' Throughout the remaining chapters, the contributors to this volume will suggest various methods of approaching this problem which are extensions of their particular treatment orientation.

In the example above, the fear of the hospital setting was handled by accepting the individual's objections at face value, and basically, avoiding the anxiety provoking situation. Solomon (Chapter 6), on the other hand, proposes that the stigma can only be alleviated by a specific admission and intake procedure, the *principles* of which are probably applicable to both outpatient and inpatient situations.

Goren (Chapter 5) indirectly proposed a solution to this problem through the hospitalization of the entire family. Here, however, efforts are made to remove the stigma of ''identified patient'' from a single family member and place the family problem in the context of the entire system. Schumann (Chapter 2), on the other hand, intimates that the stigma associated with psychiatric hospitalization may be insurmountable.

Finally, Wheeler (Chapter 4) discusses an interesting aspect of the question of social stigma, namely, that the *therapist* may have concerns about *practicing* in the psychiatric setting. Certainly, this is a possibility which deserves consideration and exploration. It would be especially significant if such an attitude prevailed across one particular treatment approach; one would then be required to question the validity of applying that approach in the psychiatric setting. To date, however, it appears that such bias is confined largely to individual therapists and does not necessarily reflect the prevailing attitude of any particular "school" or treatment orientation.

Patient centered treatment orientation or bias. The psychiatric setting traditionally emphasizes the individual as the locus of treatment. For example, Maxmen, et al. (1974) defined the hospital environment "as one in which the unit's overall structure maximally utilizes and coordinates the entire staff's efforts towards the rehabilitation of the *patient's particular behavior problems* so that ultimately he becomes a longstanding and productive member of society" (p. 33, italics added).

On the surface, this definition or orientation may not appear unique. Difficulties arise, however, when the generally accepted "systems" bias of family therapists is encountered. This view, which defines the patient's problems within the larger context of the family, is described by Minuchin (1974) who states that "the identified patient's symptoms can be assumed to be a system-maintaining or system-maintained device. The symptom may be an expression of a family dysfunction." (p. 110). In essence, the family approach has shifted the treatment focus from the *individual* to the *set of relationships* (family) in which the individual exists. In conformity with this focus, the family approach tends to de-emphasize individual developmental and intrapsychic issues through the introduction of a different language or vocabulary into the assessment and treatment process. Thus, such terms as alliances, enmeshment, subsystem and triangulation (Appendix) are commonly utilized by family therapists. It should also be pointed out that this "broader" treatment perspective has not been limited to "pure" systems theory models but is found in the behavioral (Liberman, 1970; Rappaport and Harrel, 1972), communications (Guerney, 1977; Rose, 1977) and psychodynamic (Chapter 6) approaches as well. From this perspective, then, the treatment question becomes: "Is this a 'sick' individual or a 'sick' family?" (Davies, Ellenson and Young, 1966).

Mrs. F was a 35-year-old mother of two admitted to an inpatient unit with an acute and progressive depression. She expressed intense feelings of hopelessness and helplessness; further, she indicated that these feelings were related to her ambivalence about her present marriage and her increasing sexual interest in other men. A psychiatric evaluation concluded that Mrs. F's situation was the result of unresolved oedipal conflicts involving a desire to please her father and compete with her mother. It was further hypothesized that Mrs. F was attracted to men who were reflective of her father and that a resolution of these oedipal issues would alter both Mrs. F's depression and her marital relationship. A family therapist on the unit, however, proposed a different hypothesis following assessment interviews and the administration of several self-report questionnaires. This hypothesis proposed that the contingencies of reinforcement within the marital dyad were inadequate; it was suggested that a system of negative reinforcement had replaced positive reward for desired behavior and that the reciprocal ''give'' and ''take'' relationship within the marriage had reached an imbalance. A behavior exchange treatment involving communications training and contingency contracting was proposed to improve the marital relationship and, thus, alleviate Mrs. F's depression.

Polarized views can lead to significant difficulties in the implementation of family intervention in the psychiatric setting. For example, treatment programs based exclusively on the individual may be antithetical to the inclusion of elements representing the family perspective. Indeed, this orientation may lead to viewing the family as ''outsiders'' who interfere with treatment and are both sick *and* destructive to the individual and the treatment process. Second, assessment biases may lead to the accumulation of limited data due to an overemphasis on individual or interactional variables rather than a balancing of the two perspectives (Anderson, 1977). In short, implementation of family intervention can result in a very pragmatic and practical problem: a conflict in treatment approaches on both theoretical and methodological levels.

Contributors to this volume suggest various solutions or approaches to this problem, ranging from the need for staff flexibility to the restructuring of the entire admission/treatment process. Suggestions generally recognize the necessity for some form of administrative sanction and support for the family approach as well as the need to communicate aims, goals, and methods clearly to other treatment agents involved with the patient. Readers are directed to Chapters 2 and 5 in particular, for a further explanation of the theoretical and treatment problems related to this topic.

Effects of time constraints on treatment. Most family intervention with psychiatric patients currently takes place in the context of a short-term treatment process. In the inpatient setting, this is generally defined as a period of three weeks or less (Maxmen, et al., 1974), while other psychiatric settings may provide somewhat longer treatment possibilities. In any case, treatment time is generally somewhat limited.

> M.A. was a 21-year-old, single college student admitted to an inpatient unit as the result of an acute psychotic episode characterized by feelings of persecution by his professors and beliefs that fellow students were planning to harm him and were attempting to control his thoughts and activities. On admission, M.A. stated that he was primarily concerned about his ability to complete his college curriculum. He further indicated that, although he was not particularly interested in college, he was fulfilling his parents' wishes. Both parents, he stated, were professional people with advanced academic degrees who expected their children to reach the same level of academic achievement. M.A.'s older brother was a chemical engineer and his older sister had recently graduated from law school. The family resided 400 miles from the location of M.A.'s hospitalization. The patient was admitted during summer break approximately one month prior to the resumption of school. Because of the geographical distance, only two family interviews were possible in addition to several telephone contacts. However, the primary treatment constraint involved the issue of time: both the patient and his family were adamant in their insistence that treatment be completed by the start of the fall school term. They stated that if M.A. was not released voluntarily he would leave the hospital against medical advice in order not to disrupt his educational process. Despite obvious family problems thought to be major precipitants of the patient's symptomatology, the primary treatment effort was directed toward the alleviation of M.A.'s psychotic symptoms through the administration of psychotropic medication. He was discharged in time to begin school with the recommendation that family therapy be arranged as quickly as possible to resolve problems related to family expectations.

Time constraints may have direct effects on various aspects of the treatment process, including assessment, the determination of goals and the evaluation of outcome. For example, if the average length of stay on an inpatient unit is three weeks and there is only limited access to the identified patient's family members, how does one assess more than the surface problems evident in the family system? By the same token, what kinds of goals can be set *and* accomplished within this time frame? And, finally, what can be considered reasonable measures of positive outcome in this context?

Current family intervention techniques describe a variety of anticipated goals ranging from improved communication to individuation, changes in reinforcement patterns and some form of improved family relationships. Are these reasonale goals in the psychiatric (especially the inpatient) context? Or, as Anderson (1977) asks, might the primary goal be to help the family accept outpatient family treatment *following* discharge? If it is true that "to treat a hospitalized patient in the absence of his family is to ignore an essential if not dominant aspect of his existence" (Maxmen, et al., 1974, p. 191), should this family treatment aim at the resolution of broad and basic problems? Or, should this treatment parallel that of the individual patient with the goal of "minimal remission of only the most acute and disorganizing symptoms" (Goldstein, Rodnuck, Evans, May and Steinberg) with the remainder of the treatment undertaken once the patient has left the inpatient setting?

One possibility for overcoming, at least in part, the difficulty of initial assessment and goal setting has been suggested by Withersly, Porterfield, and Spardlin (1975). Their approach in working with adolescents has been to hospitalize family members *along with* the identified patient for the initial 24-48 hours. This, however, may be quite impractical in many settings. In addition, other evidence idicates that the most crucial point of involvement for the patient's family (at least as it effects recidivism rates) is when the decision for admission is being made (Withersly, 1977).

Readers of this book will find several suggestions which should help in dealing with time constraints and their effects on treatment often imposed in the psychiatric setting.

Chronicity of identified patient and family resistance. A fourth problem frequently faced in the psychiatric setting concerns family resistance to involvement in the treatment process. This difficulty is encountered on several fronts. For example, admission to a psychiatric facility usually occurs at a time when the family demonstrates limited or decreased ability to cope with the ordinary aspects of life. This, combined with the common feelings of responsibility, fear and guilt associated with psychiatric hospitalization, often results in efforts by the family to take a stand of "non-involvement" with the identified patient's treatment. Unfortunately, this predisposition on the part of the family is often reinforced and exacerbated by initial contact with treatment staff. As pointed out previously, the family may be targeted as the "enemy" and the "cause" of the individual's principal problems. Thus, from a treatment perspective, family members may be seen as an obstacle rather than an ally in treatment. Such a situation further alienates the family and results in even less accessibility and cooperation (Appleton, 1974).

> Ms. S is a 28-year-old, single female who has been hospitalized a total of 19 times over a period of 12 years, including one four-year period at a state mental hospital. Her consistent diagnosis has been schizophrenia, paranoid type; her behavior has been marked by delusions, auditory and visual hallucinations and aggressive (largely self-destructive) outbursts. On numerous occasions, family members (her mother and siblings) have been involved in overall treatment programs based on the observation that significant deterioration in Ms. S's behavior has occurred during periods spent in the family home. During the last three inpatient hospitalizations and one treatment in partial hospitalization, family members have refused to be involved with the hospital staff. Family members have stated (with some degree of accuracy) that the patient has been hospitalized so frequently that staff has become the real family. Despite the family's essential failure to change their interactional pattern with Ms. S, they state that treatment has accomplished nothing significant; further, they are tired of the whole process. The basic request of the family is that something be done "to the patient" which will make her "fit in with the family."

Another significant condition, illustrated by the above example, which often limits the willingness of families to participate in treatment, involves the relative chronicity of the identified patient's illness or problems. With the current emphasis on short-term hospitalization and deinstitutionalization, it is not unusual to find patients undergoing multiple hospitalizations throughout the course of their illness. It is not unusual to find families gradually tiring of the entire treatment process. Having been involved in several attempts to assist the hospitalized patient, families will frequently adopt an attitude of resignation and hopelessness. This "what's-the-use" attitude, though not particularly advantageous to the patient, is understandable from the family's perspective. The net result, however, is increased family resistance to involvement in the treatment process.

Several other factors in the psychiatric setting may contribute to a lack of family involvement. For example, practices such as staff availability only during normal daytime working hours often create unnecessary hardships for families and, thus, increase resistance to participation. On the other hand, simple matters such as geographical distance, transportation difficulties or physical disabilities of particular family members may reduce the possibilities of family involvement unless these factors are openly considered in establishing treatment plans.

Finally, it should be recognized that, not infrequently, individuals treated in outpatient psychiatric settings deter family involvement themselves. Most commonly, these individuals wish to retain nearly complete secrecy about their participation in therapy; consequently, they often refuse any family contact, much less consider participation by family members in the actual therapeutic process.

To date, proponents of family treatment have clearly indicated that the key role in recruiting and involving families rests with the staffs of psychiatric facilities (Anderson, 1977; Maxmen, et al., 1974). Furthermore, they seem to be in nearly unanimous agreement that the time of initial contact is the pivotal point in establishing a productive, working relationship. How this is to be done, however, is still a relatively non-specific area. Contributors to this book suggest several possibilities ranging from taking treatment *to* the family to restructuring the process of admission to treatment in such a way that family treatment or involvement becomes an integral and necessary part of the therapeutic system.

It is this editor's judgment that widespread family intervention will become a reality only through a radical revision of our treatment perspective. This revision involves both our view of the individual and those influences contributing to the patient's problems as well as our conceptualization of the nature and efficacy of treatment itself. In the former instance, this can mean viewing the patient in a larger context than the individual's symptomatology. In the latter instance, this requires perceiving treatment as an ongoing process with the distinct possibility that the locus of treatment may have to be shifted from professional therapist to "professional" family member(s). Such a shift may, of course, require a certain demythologizing and specification of treatment interventions, which, to date, has been relatively uncommon. In this vein, Park (1978) clearly states the alternatives when she writes, "It would seem evident that the patient's family are most constructively seen, not as co-patients bemired in a shared 'family pathology' and themselves in need of therapy, but as co-providers, together with the professional team, of a milieu which will be truly therapeutic" (p. 109). The key question facing family therapists today is how to incorporate these "co-providers" into the entire therapeutic system.

Tentative emotional control of the identified patient. Another factor inhibiting the implementation of family intervention in the psychiatric setting involves the mental status and emotional stability of the hospitalized family member. This problem is highlighted by a series of case studies presented by Guttman (1973) which illustrate the potentially disruptive effects of family therapy on the identified patient.

> A 19-year-old, single male was admitted to a day hospital after demonstrating progressive lack of interest in school work and inappropriate behavior at school. Following two instances in which he entered the girl's washroom, he was expelled. In the day hospital, he was treated with phenothiazines and was seen in family therapy with his parents and 15-year-old brother. During these sessions, the father's feelings toward the boy and a seductive relationship between the boy and his mother were revealed. During this period, the patient entered his parents' bedroom twice and masturbated in their presence. His anxiety increased and he became incoherent. In addition, he began to stay away from the day hospital and from family therapy sessions. Finally, he took an overdose and was hospitalized. (Adapted from Guttman, 1973).

In this and other case studies, Guttman identifies certain characteristics, such as the inability of the individual to verbally express feelings, which contraindicate family therapy and concludes that with these characteristics present, "family therapy should be done with great caution, if at all, because the family situation heightens the identified patient's anxiety level to psychotic proportions and can ultimately precipitate a breakdown" (p. 354). Furthermore, Guttman contends that the most important factor determining therapeutic failure is "the fragility of the identified patient"; the type of family intervention provided is secondary. This brief description clearly demonstrates the dilemma frequently faced in the psychiatric setting, namely, the desire or therapeutic necessity to involve families versus the potentially destructive results of such involvement, especially for the hospitalized family member.

In light of these factors, how does one implement family intervention? What weight does the therapist give to the pathology of the hospitalized family member in designing family intervention strategies? Will these strategies have to consider the individual more carefully in the context of the total family system? And finally, are there particular family intervention models which appear more applicable and relevant to psychiatric patients than other models in light of this characteristic?

Definitive answers to these questions are not yet available. Throughout the chapters of this book, however, several suggestions are made which may prove to be quite utilitarian. One theme appears to be consistent, namely, the necessity to tailor goals to fit individual circumstances and to provide direct, structured treatment. Such approaches seem to provide at least minimal parameters and guidelines for the clinician.

Inability to be selective in choosing family types to be treated.

> An inpatient service in a psychiatric hospital has a maximum census of 25 patients. In general, it is typically staffed with medical personnel and two social workers who have the major responsibility for family work with unit patients. At any one time, the patient census represents the entire spectrum of demographic variables. Patients range in age from 16 to 70; although predominantly from lower socioeconomic levels with multiple psychiatric hospitalizations, a significant number are acute, first-hospitalization patients from middle-class families. The majority either reside with family memers or have frequent contact with families who are considered to play a significant role in their symptomatology and hospitalization. Identified patients present a diverse catalog of symptoms ranging from depression to anorexia to compulsive behavior to hallucinations, delusions and well defined, fixed paranoid ideation. In most cases, patients are admitted in an acute state with initial treatment aimed at the alleviation of overt symptoms. The average length of stay is approximately 21 days. The stated treatment philosophy of the unit includes a provision for the incorporation of family therapy during the patient's hospitalization.

In theory, all families represented by a member receiving treatment in the psychiatric setting are eligible for family therapy. Not only are these families "eligible for treatment," but from a thorough family therapy perspective their involvement is absolutely required for comprehensive treatment to be achieved. One implication of this position is that, except in those rare cases where several family intervention models are represented adequately by a diversified staff of professionals, therapists must treat families as they present themselves, with minimal opportunities to be selective regarding the types of families involved. Again, in theory, a therapist trained in a particular family therapy approach must apply that technique to all families presenting themselves for treatment.

A selection process *does* appear to exist which eliminates some families from certain types of family intervention. This process cannot always be defined as thoroughly objective in nature. For example, Evans, Chagoya, and Rakoff (1971) conducted a study designed to determine how often conjoint family therapy was actually

utilized on an adolescent psychiatric inpatient ward where the obliga-
tory policy was that *all* adolescents should be treated by this approach.
Of 100 families studied, only 50 percent received family treatment.

Obviously, valid reasons for exclusion from conjoint family
therapy were identified in this study (such as parents' refusal to participate because they had separated). At least two other factors,
however, seemed to influence involvement in therapy. On the one
hand, the findings indicated that *diagnosis* influenced whether a given
family received family treatment; the authors concluded that the
more pathology the diagnosis suggested, the less likely that the family
would receive conjoint treatment. On the other hand, *socioeconomic*
status apparently influenced inclusion or exclusion. Results suggested
that middle-class families were chosen for treatment while the poorest
families were less likely to be selected for conjoint family therapy. In
conclusion, the authors offer two suggestions worth noting. First, the
reasons for excluding families from treatment, at least in this case,
were not universally based on valid contraindications but "might well
be a comprehensive survey of the therapist's resistance to
involvement in CFT (conjoint family therapy)" (p. 106). And
second, "the data in this study suggest that the healthier families get
treated and get better, whereas the sicker families stay sick, or are
dropped, or deteriorate" (p. 107).

This study indicates that some selection processes are exercised
by therapists even in situations where family therapy is the preferred
treatment. These processes, however, may not be directly correlated
to the needs or appropriateness of treatment for particular families. It
might be speculated that in the absence of objective criteria and faced
with a variety of families, therapists eliminate families on the basis of
subjective and largely unrecognized criteria. Not the least of these
subjective criteria are the diagnosis and socioeconomic status of the
identified patient as well as the therapist's own fears, doubts, or concerns regarding the ability to provide family therapy.

In the typical psychiatric setting, it is unlikely that the selection
of families can be openly based on such criteria as diagnosis and
socioeconomic level. Unlike a private practice setting, families must
be treated as they present themselves. As Wheeler (Chapter 4) points
out, intake can not be controlled to provide a caseload of compatible
(to the therapist), high-functioning families. Thus, the therapist is
faced with several options: 1. implementing a single treatment
strategy with all families regardless of their individual differences;
2. modifying a single strategy as much as possible to account for individual needs; 3. utilizing several strategies depending on the char-

acteristics of particular families; and 4. utilizing subjective natural selection processes which will aid in eliminating certain incompatible families from treatment.

Throughout this book, several treatment approaches to families are described. Contributors discuss the types of families most suited to their particular approach or modifications which may be necessary to provide more general applicability of their treatment strategy. The psychiatric setting presents a unique problem in its involvement with a wide range of family types in the treatment process. It is hoped that some of the suggestions presented here will prove useful in providing a more coherent and objective approach to this problem.

Staff cooperation and support.

> An inpatient psychiatric unit offers a treatment program which includes medication, group, milieu, individual, and family therapy. In this program, two trainees, working as a team, treat six to eight patients on an individual basis and are responsible for evaluating and treating families of the other trainee's caseload. In this system, at least five distinct subgroups of people exist who are involved in treatment and with whom information must be shared (or withheld) in order for treatment decisions to be made. These subgroups include the patient, the family, the individual and family therapists, and the ward staff, the latter being responsible as a group for administrative decisions about patients which are considered to be binding on both the individual and family therapist, who are also expected to implement these decisions. Thus, therapeutic progress depends on open communication and unified action by the entire staff. (Boyd, 1979).

The typical psychiatric unit (whether inpatient, outpatient, or partial hospitalization) is usually composed of a multidisciplinary staff of professionals with varying backgrounds, interests, and expertise. In addition, psychiatric ward programs are generally multifaceted and composed of several elements including group, individual, and family treatments; these, in turn, may be components of a ward-wide program such as a token economy or therapeutic milieu. Coordination and integration of each of these treatment facets can be a major effort, but is a practical imperative if successful and maximal therapeutic benefits are to be achieved.

From this perspective, it is important that any form of family intervention initiated within the context of a psychiatric treatment program be an integrated segment of that program rather than an independent treatment component. It is necessary, also, that staff implementing family treatment be integrated into, and familiar with, other facets of the total treatment program. In addition, family thera- pists frequently view the patient from a different perspective than other staff members. And finally, family treatment may involve the implementation of a particular technique in the hospital which must then be taught to, and carried out within, the family setting following discharge.

All of these factors indicate the practical necessity of treatment coordination and staff cooperation. Unfortunately, these steps are not always easily achieved. As various contributors will illustrate throughout this book, detrimental effects often result from inade- quate communication among staff regarding outcome in separate program components. For example, the family therapist may be uninformed regarding events taking place with a particular patient in group therapy. In a similar way, conflict and resistance can develop around the introduction of a treatment perspective or technique which is unfamiliar to staff members (such as requiring a consistent response from staff to a particular patient behavior because that re- sponse will be reproduced in the family setting following discharge).

Problems related to staff cooperation and administrative support for the implementation of family therapy are discussed in subsequent chapters. In addition, Anderson (Chapter 7) summarizes and dis- cusses these issues in detail. As Rabiner, Molinski and Gralnick (1962) point out, the involvement of the family in the treatment pro- cess can be advantageous to staff both as an aid in predicting stresses and problems the patient will face on the return to home and as a possible source for generalizing treatment procedures following dis- charge. It appears, therefore, that adequate solutions to the problems of staff cooperation and treatment integration must be sought and implemented in order to potentiate the positive effects of family treatment.

Difficulty maintaining continuity of care. One of the persistent prob- lems faced by therapists in the psychiatric setting is the provision of continuing care for patients and families. Basically, his problem in- volves the continuation of treatment in a consistent manner as the patient moves from one treatment setting to another.

T.P. was a 27-year-old, separated female who had been hospi- talized in an inpatient service on two previous occasions and was currently being treated in a partial hospitalization program. She had completed three years of college and desired to return to complete her degree in elementary education. On admission, she verbalized three basic problem areas: a feeling of rejection by her parents, both of whom were divorced, remarried, and de- sired little contact with the patient; ambivalence regarding her husband who had deserted her three years previously and whose whereabouts were unknown at the time of admission; and anxiety in a variety of school situations, especially those related to tests and test-taking. Treatment was directed toward aiding the patient develop as satisfactory a relationship with her parents as possible given the realities of the situation and their unavailability and unwillingness to participate in treatment; initiating divorce proceedings from her husband to resolve her ambivalent situation, and initiation of desensitization procedures. The patient was discharged after three months and returned to school with the recommendation that continued treatment be obtained to solidify gains made in the problem areas mentioned. Unfortunately, the only services available to the patient on return to school were those of the college counseling service. Contact with this service revealed that, although they were concerned with the student's continued treatment, severely limited resources made more than periodic monitoring of the patient impossible. The closest comprehensive psychiatric facility was located 50 miles from T.P.'s school. This facility expressed willingness to provide service if the individual could provide her own transportation; T.P., however, had no car and no regular public transportation was available between the two locations. The only concrete resolution that could be achieved was the indication of the school counseling service that every effort would be made to provide the patient with continued treatment.

It has been postulated that for many patients "the major function of psychiatric hospitalization should be preparing for aftercare" (Maxmen, et al., 1974, p. 209). More specifically, the aim of inpatient hospitalization should be to develop and sustain those behaviors which will make the patient most compatible with the environment outside the hospital. Frequently, of course, this aim can only be *initiated* during hospitalization, resulting in the necessity to continue treatment following discharge. As mentioned previously, in this situation, the family can be conceptualized as one agent which can be mobilized to perform this task.

The family cannot be enlisted, however, as "co-providers" of treatment (Park, 1978) on the final day of hospitalization. On the contrary, as Wheeler (Chapter 4) and Solomon (Chapter 6) point out, family involvement must be initiated at the beginning of treatment and must continue throughout the entire therapeutic process. If this procedure is not followed, it is highly unlikely that a workable alliance with the family can be achieved.

Unfortunately, this last minute recruitment of family members is not unusual. Often, under the pressures of time, large caseloads, and inadequate staffing patterns, treatment agents fail to incorporate family members into the planning process until they are faced with the imminent discharge of the patient. At this point, the family becomes "the last resort" in aftercare treatment. A smooth and effective continuity of treatment is difficult under such circumstances.

An additional difficulty is presented in providing continuing professional care following discharge. Despite the inherent disadvantages and problems, inpatient family therapists have certain advantages over their outpatient counterparts. First, they are able to exert more control over patient-family contact; second, they are able to utilize multiple treatment techniques or modalities in treating the patient; and finally, they are able to have more direct control over the extent to which treatment will be patient-centered or family-centered (Maxmen, Tucker, and LeBow, 1974). Once the patient moves from the inpatient setting, management of these elements of treatment becomes less centralized and more difficult. Frequently, for example, individual and family programs will be fragmented since different therapists perform these treatment functions. This situation, of course, raises the same problems of staff cooperation and treatment coordination described previously.

A third area of difficulty in providing continuity of care arises in the transition from outpatient to inpatient treatment. This problem frequently results from divergent perspectives regarding the function of the two modalities. On the one hand, outpatient staff see themselves as primary treatment planners and providers. From this perspective, should hospitalization be required, it is considered as merely one step in the continuum of treatment; as such, the inpatient treatment should be directed toward implementing the basic outpatient treatment plan which has already been constructed. On the other hand, inpatient staff often view their primary responsibility as that of assessing the patient's current functioning and developing an adequate treatment plan to improve this functioning. They then expect that once the patient is discharged, this plan will be carried out by outpatient treatment agents.

Unfortunately, much of this conflict results from the imposition of value systems and treatment biases inherent with therapists. As pointed out above, these biases provide a natural selection process for screening out families who are inappropriate for treatment. Put in its most blatant form, "those (families) who are 'allowed' to continue treatment longest are those families which prove to be interesting to us because of their similarity to the therapist's own middle-class situation" (Shellow, Brown, and Osberg, 1963).

In other ways, also, therapist value systems affect continuity of care. For example, often, therapists are hesitant to recognize the actual qualifications of other providers or the inherent qualities of other treatment settings in determining and arranging continuing care. Too frequently, the desires of the individuals or families being treated are ignored because of professional biases and value systems.

In essence, then, we sometimes find two different modalities conceptualizing and implementing plans which are expected to be carried out regardless of who may be the primary treatment providers at the time. This situation, of course, gives rise to multiple problems involving competition between modalities, questions regarding primary responsibility for treatment planning, and even greater difficulty in insuring the continuity of care.

Summary

This chapter has reviewed some of the indicators which demonstrate the growth of family involvement in both research and practice. It has further indicated that along with this growth has come a proliferation of approaches, orientations, or "schools" of family therapy. These approaches, in turn, have been increasingly applied to patients and their families seen in the psychiatric setting. Attendant to this application has been an increasing awareness that the psychiatric setting poses unique problems which may have significant implications for the implementation of family therapy. Finally, each of these problems has been briefly reviewed to provide a context in which to view the following chapters of this volume.

Chapters 2 through 6 present five different approaches to family therapy including systems, communications training, behavior modification, and structural and dynamic orientations. The authors of these chapters describe the theoretical basis of their approaches and then apply the approach to the hospital setting with special emphasis on the inpatient unit. In addition, each contributor gives attention to the problems outlined in this chapter and the implications for their treatment orientation.

In Chapter 7, Carol Anderson delineates the practical problems and issues which arise when attempting to integrate family intervention within a setting which is predominantly oriented around the medical model. Strategies are suggested to facilitate this process on both technical and political levels. Specific examples are used to illustrate these issues.

Finally, the Appendix to this volume includes short descriptions or examples of techniques which have been utilized by various theoretical orientations in family interventions. They are intended as illustrations and guides for the clinician in implementing family strategies.

References

Anderson, C. A. Family intervention with severely disturbed patients. *Archives of General Psychiatry*, 1977, *34*, 697-702.

Appleton, W. S. Mistreatment of patients' families by psychiatrists. *American Journal of Psychiatry*, 1974, *131*, 655-657.

Boyd, J. H. The interaction of family therapy and psychodynamic individual therapy in an inpatient setting. *Psychiatry*, 1979, *43*, 99-110.

Davies, D. J., Ellenson, G. & Young, R. Therapy with a group of families in a psychiatric day center. *American Journal of Orthopsychiatry*, 1966, *36*, 134-146.

DeWitt, K. The effectiveness of family therapy. *Archives of General Psychiatry*, 1978, *35*, 549-561.

Evans, H. A., Chagoya, L., & Rakoff, V. Decision-making as to the choice of family therapy in an adolescent inpatient setting. *Family Process*, 1971, *10*, 97-109.

Goldstein, M. J., Rednick, E. H., Evans, J. R. & Steinberg, M. Drug and family therapy in the aftercare treatment of acute schizophrenia. *Archives of General Psychiatry*, 1978, *35*, 1169-1177.

Gould, E. & Glick, D. The effects of family presence and brief family intervention on global outcome for hospitalized schizophrenic patients. *Family Process*, 1977, *16*, 503-510.

Gould, E. & Glick, D. Families, family therapy and schizophrenia in an inpatient setting: A one year follow-up, unpublished manuscript, Langley-Porter Neuropsychiatric Institute, 1976.

Group for the Advancement of Psychiatry. The field of family therapy. *Reports and Symposiums*, 1970, *7*, 525-644.

Guerney, B. G. *Relationship enhancement: Skill-training programs for therapy, problem prevention, and enrichment,* San Francisco: Jossey-Bass, 1977.

Gurman, A. S. & Kniskern, D. P. Deterioration in marital and family therapy: Empirical, clinical, and conceptual issues. *Family Process*, 1978, *17*, 3-20.

Gurman, A. S. & Rice, D. G. (Eds). *Couples in conflict: New directions in marital therapy.* New York: Aronson, 1975.

Guttman, H. A. A contraindication for family therapy. *Archives of General Psychiatry*, 1973, *29*, 352-355.

Lee, A. R. & Mayerson, S. Inpatient individual and family therapy of adult schizophrenic patients without drugs. Unpublished manuscript, Emanuel Mental Health Center, Turlock, CA, 1973.

Liberman, R. Behavioral approaches to family and couple therapy. *American Journal of Orthopsychiatry,* 1970, *40,* 106-118.

Luber, R. F. Teaching models in marital therapy: A review and research issue. *Behavior Modification,* 1978, *2,* 77-91.

Lubin, B., Reddy, W., Taylor, A. & Lubin, A. The group psychotherapy literature: 1977. *International Journal of Group Psychotherapy,* 1978, *28,* 509-555.

Mash, E. J., Hamerlynck, L. A. & Handy, L. C. *Behavior modification and families.* NY: Brunner/Mazel, 1976.

Maxmen, J., Tucker, G. & LeBow, W. *Rational hospital psychiatry.* NY: Brunner/Mazel, 1974.

Minuchin, S. *Families and family therapy.* Cambridge, MA: Harvard University Press, 1974.

Park, C. C. Partial hospitalization and family involvement: A family member's perspective. In R. Luber, J. Maxey and P. Lefkovitz, (Eds.) *Proceedings of the annual conference on partial hospitalization: 1977.* Boston: Federation of Partial Hospitalization Study Groups, 1978.

Parloff, M. and Dies, R. Group Psychotherapy outcome research 1966-1975. *International Journal of Group Psychotherapy,* 1977, *27,* 281-319.

Rabiner, E. L., Molinski, H., & Gralnick, A. Conjoint family therapy in the inpatient setting. *American Journal of Psychotherapy,* 1962, *16,* 618-631.

Rabkin, J. Public attitudes toward mental illness: A review of the literature. *Schizophrenia Bulletin,* 1974, *10,* 9-33.

Rappaport, A. F. & Harrel, J. E. A behavioral exchange model for marital counseling. *The Family Coordinator,* 1972, *21,* 203-212.

Rose, S. D. Group therapy: *A behavioral approach.* Englewood Cliffs, NJ: Prentice-Hall, 1977.

Shellow, R. S., Brown, B. S. & Osberg, J. W. Family group therapy in retrospect: Four years and sixty families. *Family Process,* 1963, *2,* 52-67.

Skynner, A. C. R. *Systems of family and marital psychotherapy.* NY: Brunner/Mazel, 1976.

Welch, W. M. (Ed.). *Mental Health Reports.* Plus Publications, Inc., 1979, *3* (9), May 2.

Wells, R. & Dezen, A. The results of family therapy revisited: The non-behavioral methods. *Family Process,* 1978, *17,* 251-288.

Withersly, D. J., Portersfield, P. B., & Spradlin, W. W. Treating the hospitalized adolescent—a family approach. *Family Therapy,* 1975, *2,* 129-135.

Chapter 2

THE BOWEN THEORY AND THE HOSPITALIZED PATIENT

Morton D. Schumann

EDITOR'S COMMENTS

It is possible that Murray Bowen has been the most influential figure in the field of family therapy over the last 25 years. Certainly, he must be regarded as one of the key figures responsible for the emergence of a conceptual and theoretical framework which has distinguished family therapy from the individual and group approaches. In addition, Bowen's name has become almost synonymous with the application of "systems theory" to the conceptualization and practice of family therapy, although this latter situation has, in recent years, been a source of irritation and dissatisfaction for Bowen.

In the evolutionary development of his theory, Bowen has attempted to cast family therapy concepts in a scientific framework. He began his theoretical development in the psychoanalytic tradition. Within a relatively short period, however, Bowen found that the assumptions and concepts of this approach presented conceptual problems which he considered to be prohibitively restrictive. Consequently, Bowen began to explore biology, evolution and the natural sciences in search of a broader theoretical perspective. His initial research explorations involved the mother-child symbiosis as a small "system" which had larger extensions in the family unit.

Eventually, Bowen settled on biological concepts as a means of describing human behavior; this language and framework became the cornerstone of "family systems theory," the name initially given to Bowen's theoretical construct. This system attempts to convert "subjectivity into observable and verifiable research facts" (Bowen, 1976, p. 63).

According to Bowen, "My theory is a specific theory about the functional facts of emotional functioning" (Bowen, 1976, p. 62). The core of the approach involves the ability of people to distinguish between the *feeling* process and the *intellectual* process. For Bowen, the emotional and intellectual systems are basic biological functions; humans share the former with all lower forms of life while the latter distinguishes humans from these life forms. The *feeling* system, according to Bowen, "is postulated as a link between the emotional and intellectual systems through which certain emotional states are represented in conscious awareness" (Bowen, 1976, p. 60). This theory, then, forms the basis for a method of therapy, a method which Bowen considers to be superior to traditional practices.

In recent years, Bowen has exerted some effort to relabel his approach from "family systems theory" to the "Bowen Theory." This effort has been due, at least in part, to the increased popularity of the construct and Bowen's desire to retain a distinct identity for his position. Specifically, Bowen believes that the term "family systems theory" has become overly identified and confused with "general systems theory" (which he contends has no *specific* application to emotional functioning). In addition, Bowen maintains that the term "family systems theory" has been overused, popularized and, thus, become nonspecific. Bowen contends that his theory has a specific biological rather than a general systems theory etiology. In contrast to this apparent effort at differentiation, Bowen also maintains that his theory is not unique. Indeed, he states that,

> The Bowen theory contains no ideas that have not been a part of human experience through the centuries. The theory operates on an order of facts so simple and obvious that everyone knew them all the time. The uniqueness of the theory has to do with the facts that are included, and the concepts that are specifically excluded (Bowen, 1976, p. 64).

Where does the "Bowen Theory" stand in relation to other theories and methods of family therapy? Bowen, himself, has attempted to delineate some similarities and differences (Bowen, 1978, a,b,c). In addition, he has indicated that one of the distinct advantages of his approach is that therapists can choose to incorporate parts of the system into their therapy if they are unwilling or unable to adopt the whole. In other words, from Bowen's perspective it appears that "a little systems thinking is better than none at all."

The pervasiveness of the Bowen perspective will become apparent in many chapters in this book. For example, there is rudimentary "systems thinking" evident in the behavioral approach to family therapy. Here, instead of being couched in biological terms, the theoretical concepts are in the rubrick of learning theory. Nevertheless, such concepts and methods as reinforcement, generalization, and contracting reflect a basic, but largely undeveloped systems potential. Behaviorists have moved away from the strictly operant approach in recent years but there appear to be some indications that this movement could be in the general direction of a more "systems" oriented perspective (Luber, 1978; Weiss, 1978). This movement is also seen in the somewhat reluctant but, nevertheless, gradual acceptance of "cognitive" meanings, labels and structures (O'Leary & Turkewitz, 1978) and in the theoretical and methodological development of communications training techniques of therapy (Chapter 3). It should be remembered, however, that from the generally accepted behavioral perspective, the identified patient is considered the "deviant" family member who must be "retrained." Interestingly, Bowen, himself, indicates that the behavioral approach can be effective but that change produced is usually short term; for Bowen, permanent change occurs *only* with the modification of intensity at the emotional level. Obviously, this is an area of questionable validity for the behavioral approach due to the difficulty of quantification and specification involved.

Strong systems influences are also seen in the structural approach to family therapy. In this approach, a strong present orientation is emphasized; it is postulated that symptoms persist due to the actions of the family system in the present. From the structural perspective, the therapeutic task is to elicit a new sequence of behaviors within the entire family system. Although both the Bowen Theory and structural approaches avoid focusing on so-called intrapsychic forces, there is a significant difference between the two theoretical constructs. On the one hand, the structural approach tends to view intrapsychic forces in the context of the entire relationship system; change is achieved by altering the system as a *whole*. On the other hand, the Bowen Theory advocates the modification of the relationship system through the modification of the part the *individual* plays in that system.

Finally, although he began his work within the psychoanalytic framework, Bowen has not been positively disposed toward the approach over the years. Bowen considers Freud's two monumental contributions to be the definition of emotional illness as the product of disturbed relationships, and, the discovery and conceptualization of the therapeutic relationship. These concepts are of significance in the Bowen Theory of family therapy but have been expanded and built upon extensively. Indeed, Bowen's major criticism of the dynamic approach is that it has become a "closed system" because Freud's successors accepted these two contributions as "basic truths" and became unwilling to incorproate new information into their conceptual framework. As Bowen writes:

> Functionally, it was a closed belief system equivalent to the religions, the philosophies, and the dogmas that are used on *truth* but which are unable to generate new knowledge from within nor permit new knowledge from without (Bowen, 1978c, p. 391).

Objectively, it should be noted that modifications of the more traditional dynamic approach have begun to appear in the family therapy field. The word "system" is more common in the psychoanalytic literature and it appears that some new knowledge is, indeed, penetrating this closed system. The reader is directed to Chapter 6 for an example of this development.

The following chapter presents an overview of the Bowen Theory and its application to psychiatric patients. In addition to presenting some of the basic constructs of the approach, the author delineates some of the problems faced in the implementation of the approach in the hospital setting, some of the techniques that can be utilized, and some of the family types for which the treatment is most applicable. The latter is a most importa. t consideration in light of current emphases on the field.

Raymond F. Luber

Introduction

The phrase "family therapy" has been used by mental health professionals for approximately two decades. There remains a great diversity of opinion among practitioners regarding the nature of family therapy. A report issued in March, 1970 by the Family Committee of the Group for the Advancement of Psychiatry discussed at length the state of family therapy as it seemed at that time

(GAP, 1970). The authors of that report stated "family therapy, as such, however, has only more recently begun to be clearly defined, not only as a method of treatment but also as a theoretical orientation toward psychiatric problems." The report then proceeded to demonstrate how unclearly defined family therapy was at the time. In discussing goals of therapy, it demonstrated wide diversity; in discussing indications and contraindications, it also demonstrated wide diversity. The chapter on techniques and practices illustrated an abundance of divergence in those areas; and, finally, in discussing family theory, the report stated "the meaning of family theory is, of course, complex and difficult to define."

The primary reason family theory was, and still is, difficult to define is that there is no single theory that explains or delineates what causes families to function well or what factors bring about family dysfunction. A number of practitioners have offered theoretical hypotheses but no one theory is more generally accepted than the others. There is little in the family therapy literature to indicate that valid research has been done comparing the efficacy of the theories or even substantiating the efficacy of any one theory.

One of the pioneer theoreticians in the field is Murray Bowen. The formal development of the Bowen Theory began with his NIMH research project in the 1950s (Bowen, 1961). This project, reported at the American Orthopsychiatric Association meeting in 1959, consisted of a hospital psychiatric ward in which adult psychiatric patients and their normal parents lived in a continuing observation and treatment situation. The family was the unit of treatment, and all the family members attended all the psychotherapy hours together.

In the 20 years following the NIMH project, the Bowen Theory has emerged from an anomalous position in the family field and in psychiatry to a position of greater respect and acceptance. Throughout these years Bowen has constantly refined and further defined the theory as his experiences in working with families have provided him with keener insights and sharper delineations of family relationship systems. What has transpired, however, is that Bowen has moved from a base within a hospital setting to a predominantly out-patient practice, and the resultant theory is not particularly applicable to family intervention with hospitalized patients. As in any two-person relationship conflict, each component contributes to the function, to the dysfunction, or to the non-function of the relationship component. No single component is totally responsible for the outcome, yet each, because of its individual developmental history, genetic structure, and societal expectation, contributes to a denouement of incisive compatibility or incompatibility. Such a situation exists in the relationship between the hospital setting and the Bowen Theory. To understand the basis of this conflict, it is first necessary to examine the conceptual structure of the Bowen Theory as well as the operational behavior philosophy of psychiatric treatment in hospital settings.

Medical Model Issues

The practice of medicine pre-dates the Christian era by thousands of years. The causes of illness, have with the passage of time, been attributed to many and various determinants. Medical practitioners, whether they are witch doctors in their huts of mud and grass, or highly skilled specialists who lope through the glass and concrete multi-floored hospitals of urban America, have for thousands of years shared at least one belief: that the illness a person experiences is within that person and the treatment of the illness, therefore, must be directed at that person.

Psychiatry, as a branch of medicine dealing with emotional or behavioral disorders, has also postulated that the individual is the unit of treatment. The practice of psychiatry in hospitals, at one point in its history, was so embued with the concept of the individual that people labeled "patients" were frequently removed from their families and communities and sent to isolated treatment facilities resulting in little or no contact with the family by either the patient or the hospital staff. Families were considered important only when the institution wished to make disposition of the patient. In more recent years, the family has been accepted as an important aspect of the treatment process, but more as an adjunct to the therapy of the patient rather than as the focus of treatment itself.

A major problem of hospital staffs is one basic to all systems—resistance to change. "We have always treated patients this way, why should we change, especially to a more troublesome way"? What is sometimes considered most troublesome are the relatives of patients. Because of their individual orientation to treatment, many of those who work in hospitals have developed negative reactions to patients' families. "They get in the way," "They ask too many questions," "They care less about the patient's well-being than we do," are examples of some of the ways staff rationalize their attitudes. Attitudes such as these, even where there is a verbalized commitment to a family approach, make it difficult to establish the family as the unit of treatment. Attitudes linger long after there is verbal acquiescence or intellectual agreement, so at the slightest problem, institutional staffs shift back to their old ways giving verification to the addage that "the more things change the more they remain the same."

Another issue affecting family treatment is economic. Even when medical and hospital staffs accept family therapy as a valid method of treatment, in this world of third party payors, there may be a struggle to receive payment for their efforts. The question of family treatment constituting medical treatment is one that has created acrid debate between family practitioners and insurance carriers. Many of the latter refuse to pay for family therapy; thus, it is necessary for one member to be designated as "patient" in order for the therapist to be compensated for his time even though there may be equal amounts of "pathology" in other family members.

Perhaps the factor hindering the use of family therapy in a hospital setting most is the admission of a person to the hospital. This action *ipso facto* proclaims that person to be the sick one, regardless of what the attitude or treatment philosophy of the hospital and staff may be, the family of the person will, in the majority of instances, continue to respond to that person as the "sick one." Additionally, the family will have great difficulty accepting the idea that any other person or relationship has more than a superficial bearing on the maintenance of the illness. It is their belief, and the hospitalization proves to them, that the illness is in the person labeled "patient."

Essential to the Bowen Theory is the belief that the family, not the individual, is the unit of treatment. Hospitalization bars the effective application of this belief and subverts the use of other concepts of the theory. Experiences of numerous family therapists tend to affirm the incompatibility of the two models.

Based on his experience in attempting to establish a family unit as an independent service in a community mental health clinic, Framo (1976) questioned whether a systems model of therapy can be integrated with an individual illness model. He cites differences in premise, philosophy, and orientation as estopping factors.

The fact that the application of the Bowen theoretical approach may be subverted by hospitalization does not rule out the consideration of parts of the theory in specific situations. Even in individual treatment it is necessary for the therapist to keep in mind that the patient is a subsystem. If the therapist fails to do this then therapy, too, is in danger of subversion. A system is made up of components and the relationship between the components. Change in any component or relationship requires the system to operate differently than prior to the change. Bowen speaks of working with the healthiest part of the family system. If that part changes, then the entire family system functions differently.

Bowen's early papers and the video-teaching tapes he produced while associated with the Medical College of Virginia described his theory as being composed of six concepts: differentiation of self, triangles, nuclear family emotional system, the family projection process, the multi-generational transmission process, and sibling position (Bowen, 1966, 1968).

More recently, two additional concepts have been added: the emotional cut-off and societal regression (Bowen, 1976, 1978). Emotional cut-off is primarily a refinement of a phenomenological description of behavior frequently encountered in family systems. Societal regression refers to the extension of family theory to societal problems. Neither of these concepts nor the concept of sibling position is more than peripherally germaine to the major topic at hand. Consequently, they will not be discussed further in this chapter.

Although the concepts listed above are separate and unique, each impacts on, and intertwines with the other to constitute the matrix from which the Bowen Theory emerges. Certain aspects of each concept which I believe affect the utilization of the theory in hospital settings follow.

Differentiation of Self

The concept of differentiation of self is concerned with making specific intellectual functioning separate from emotional reactiveness. The behavior of most persons is determined by two fundamental processes, feelings and the emotional response to those feelings; and thinking and the actions resulting from such cognitive process. In all persons, there is a fusion of these two processes; the resultant lifestyle of a person depends on which process is dominant. Where emotional functioning dominates, thought processes are blocked out. Such a person then becomes one who is a reactor; the life course is side-tracked by reactions to whatever affects the person emotionally. The person whose intellect is dominant proceeds on course toward a life goal which has been thoughtfully planned regardless of the manner in which the emotions might be confronted.

An illustration of this are persons who, on experiencing a difference of opinion with their boss, quit their job in a huff, then are without income for several months until forced to take an inferior position in order to support themselves and their families. These people are reacting on an emotional basis. The non-reactors might conclude that because of the difference of opinion the job may not be for them, but remain there until locating another job consonant with previously established goals.

As a means of explaining this process Bowen devised a "scale of differentiation of self." This scale describes all human behavior as lying on a continuum between 0 and 100. Those persons at the lower end function in response to feelings; those at the higher end function in response to a cognitive process. The goal of those at the lower end is to feel good, feel comfortable. They go along with the crowd; they may sacrifice a part of their self to be accepted, to be liked. They adopt and accept as truth the beliefs of others without questioning and without complaint.

Those at the higher end of the scale are those who do not accept an idea because someone in authority says it is so. They question, they confront, they think through, they ask for the evidence. They ask of themselves, "What do I beleive and why do I believe it?" They may end up accepting the same belief that someone at the other end of the scale accepts, but they have arrived at that belief through a process of self involvement rather than through a no-self acceptance. They know what they, as human beings, stand for and are aware of what they, as persons, believe. Frequently, people at this end of the scale have beliefs different from the majority and are considered anomalies by society in general. Often, the anomaly of one generation becomes the dogma of future generations.

Differentiation of self involves two kinds of differentiation. The first is within the self: making specific emotional processes separate from the intellect. The second process has to do with the total self of one person being capable of functioning as a distinct entity independent of other selves or combination of selves. Bowen has referred to a fused combination of selves in the family system as a "undifferentiated family ego mass." The same concept, when applied to other systems or institutions, might be called an undifferentiated university ego mass or hospital or cult. In short, "undifferentiated ego mass" is any system wherein emotional functioning operates as a bar to the exercise of individual freedom and intellect.

Triangles

Bowen views triangles as "the basic building block of any emotional system." He believes the triangle to be the smallest stable relationship system. "A two-person system may be stable as long as it is calm but when anxiety increases, it immediately involves the most vulnerable other person to become a triangle. When tension in the triangle is too great for the threesome it involves others to become a series of interlocking triangles" (Bowen, 1976, p. 76).

In a triangle, there is a more or less comfortable relationship between two persons and an uncomfortable one with the third. The latter is on the outside attempting to experience comfort with one of the members of the twosome. At such time as the tension between the twosome increases, one will reach out to the third and become allied with him. This, then, puts the other original member of the twosome in the outsider position. This process is operational in all relationship systems to some degree. Persons with relatively good levels of differentiation of self are able to adjust to the shifts without being defeated by them. The lower the level of differentiation of self in the components, the more pathological the result. The commonly perceived scapegoat phenomenon is a manifestation of this process.

An example of this process is a couple who were married for a number of years. The wife assumed the role of over-functioner in the relationship and the husband a more passive, under-functioner role. As tension mounted in the relationship, she entered into an affair with a professional counselor who roomed in their home. As their relationship blossomed, they both began to verbally attack the husband, by pointing out his inadequacies as a husband, parent, and breadwinner. This resulted in his withdrawing more and more from the relationship until the wife, on the advice of her counselor-paramour, applied to a local clinic to seek help for her "sick" husband. An appointment for the couple was given; to this first clinic visit came husband, wife, and paramour, with the wife insisting that her lover's presence was necessary to explain to the family therapist at the clinic the "sick" behavior of her husband.

The geodesic dome and the hospital system are probably two of the world's finest examples of interlocking triangles. Unlike the dome where the triangles result in a positive function, hospital system triangles, more often than not, hinder function. The number of these triangles is countless. Some of the broader examples of hospital triangles are:

- Hospital administration-doctor-patient
- Family-doctor-patient
- Family-hospital administrator-patient
- Third party carrier-hospital administration-patient
- Doctor-patient-hospital personnel

- Doctor-patient-social worker
- Social worker-patient-family.

In any one of these triangles, two sides may align against the third, not necessarily by design, but as the result of the attitudes, expectations, needs, and philosophies each brings to the relationship. Destructive triangles are extremely prevalent where a psychiatric service lacks strong leadership or the staff is otherwise disgruntled about pay, working conditions, or other work based factors that may affect their personal lives. The staff of typical hospitals either lack awareness of triangulation when it takes place, or are not constituted in such a way as to be able to deal with it administratively or within the treatment program. As a result, someone in the system (more often than not the patient) ends up in the familiar scapegoat position.

The Nuclear Family Emotional System

The functioning of a nuclear family emotional system depends on the level of differentiation in the nuclear family. According to Bowen, a person picks as a spouse another person who has a similar level of differentiation, someone who would be at the same spot on the scale of differentiation of self. The lower the level of differentiation, the greater the fusion. This fusion leads to the creation of symptoms of one, or perhaps several of the following types: marital conflict; illness in one spouse (physical or emotional illness or social dysfunction such as drinking); or the projection of the problem on children when the unstable relationship of the parents requires a triangle in order to calm the relationship. Usually, one child is more fused to the parental emotional system than the other children, but in some families where the amount of differentiation is large, several, or perhaps all, of the children may be involved to varying degrees.

In some families, one child may be seriously impaired and the others may be relatively untouched. An example of this is the family treated following a suicide attempt by a 17-year-old son. The parents were married during World War II. The father who came from a small town in the Southwest married a young woman from the Southeast while he was stationed at a training base near her home. At the war's end he took his wife to live close to his parents. She was not well liked nor well received by his large, extended family. She perceived herself to be, and was, treated like an outsider. She felt lonely and depressed for several years until she became pregnant. From that point on, her feelings and fantasies focused on the being that was growing inside her womb. By the time the child was born, a lifetime pattern of togetherness was established between mother and son. His life became her life. She involved herself in whatever he did. He, in turn, surrendered his "self" to her. By the time he reached his teens, and attempted to differentiate a self as is normal in the teenage process, he was unable to do so. This struggle became so intense that in his view he could be independent only by destroying himself. The other children, born when the marriage was more stable, and not involved in an emotional fusion with either parent, led relatively well-adjusted lives.

The Family Projection Process

In any single family system, there is a dynamic field of emotional energy. In those families that we see clinically, the energy becomes locked into a fixed system reminiscent of a zone defense in basketball. The action can shift from one side of the court to the other, from front to back, but the zone defense remains a zone. In a family system, the focus of the emotional energy shifts in three predictable zones. At times when the action is in one zone, there may be little activity in the others, but there is always the potential for the action to shift to the other zones. In families, this shifting, locked in, or undifferentiated emotional process results in dysfunctional zones or areas.

Action in one zone can result in the employment of a certain number of units of emotional energy in the creation of conflict between spouses; or a number of energy units may be directed at the maintenance and support of a physical, emotional, or social illness in the husband/wife axis. In other instances, energy may be directed to the child zone resulting in impairment of one or more children. The process can maintain a dynamic quality, constantly shifting about the mother-father-child triangle, or it can become static and deposit a proportionately large number of units on one side of the triangle or on one corner. The person or relationship on whom the emotional field is statically focused then becomes the site of primary emotional impairment in the family system. The system projects the dysfunction to one member, generally the least powerful person in the system.

When the impairment rests in a child, the projection process according to Bowen, results from the maternal instinct as governed by the mother's anxiety. The case of the suicidal teenager described earlier is an example of this type of projection process. Although the roots of the process lie in the mother-child relationship, the father is very much a part of it. His contribution arises from his insensitivity to the mother's anxiety and his inability to deal with it in a differentiated manner.

To foster change in this type of problem it is necessary to involve the entire family in the therapeutic hour. Three relationship factors must be dealt with:

- The son must be helped to differentiate a self free of the emotional bonding with his mother.
- The mother must be helped to become aware of and understand the role she plays in her son's problem without being made to feel she is to blame for the problem.
- The father must be helped to recognize the phantom role that he plays by maintaining the outside position, perhaps as a means of avoiding dealing with his wife's anxieties himself.

This type of approach is more likely to be successfully accomplished where one therapist deals with the total family and in the therapeutic session works with the various relationship systems simultaneously.

Multi-generational Transmission Process

"It seemed to me that emotional illness is a deeper phenomenon that can be explained by disturbed relationship in a single generation" (Bowen, 1976). Bowen's statement exemplifies the basic thought behind the development of the multi-generational transmission process concept. The concept itself is a blend of two other concepts, differentiation of self and the family projection process. If you were to start with parents in any given generation at a specific point on the scale of differentiation of self, take into account the hypothesis that in each succeeding generation one child will function at a lower level of differentiation, that those persons whose functioning placed them at the extreme low end of the scale are the emotionally impaired of society, then it follows that it is only a matter of time before one generation of a given family will produce an offspring so low on the scale of differentiation as to be functioning at a schizophrenic level.

In his early papers and lectures Bowen spoke of this as being a three generation process. Through the years he has altered this position so that today he speaks of it as being a more drawn out process extending over as many as eight or ten generations. The reason for this change, according to Bowen, is that the process does not proceed at the same rate of speed through all the generations. It may accelerate in some and slow down in others. The end result, whether it be in the seventh, ninth or tenth generation, is a level of impairment that is comparable to schizophrenia.

At times when I have discussed this concept in lectures, there is usually one student who will ask, "Then doesn't this mean that eventually the entire world will be peopled by schizophrenics?" Although some critics of society may believe we have already approached that level, the answer is "not necessarily." Even though one child in a family may function at a lower level than the parents, other children may not. They may function at the same or higher levels by virtue of the process moving up the scale instead of down, being less impaired by the family emotional system and, thus, providing the world with a core of more highly differentiated individuals.

A system is composed of components and the relationships among the components. Change in either a component or a relationship in the system will change the system. If a patient or any other key person in the patient's family can be engaged in a successful effort to change, then that family system changes. If the effort toward change is directed at greater differentiation then the system will function at a higher or more mature level. Unfortunately, not all patients or their families possess this capacity.

Patients who are hospitalized are, for the most part, persons who function at the lower end of the scale of differentiation of self. These are the victims of the family projection process and are outsiders in the family triangle. Many of these are diagnosed as schizophrenic or function at a level consonant with schizophrenia. Not all schizophrenic family systems function in the same manner. Consequently, not all can be treated in the same way. Two of the more frequently seen types are what might be called the "schizophrenic family" and the "family with a schizophrenic member." The lifestyle and coping capacity of each is vastly different.

In a schizophrenic family, all members of the nuclear family function at a very low level. Adjustments in all areas of living are tenuous. There is no person in the system with enough strength to anchor the system. The system is either financially indigent or marginal at best. Communication patterns are confused, and there is no evidence of closeness. This family resembles what Lidz (1973) describes as the schizmatic family. It is my opinion that this type of family presents an unworkable model for the Bowen Theory.

In order for the Bowen concepts to be utilized, there needs to be a healthy component in the system. In the schizophrenic family, no one person has a significant amount of self to be able to put change into the system. Theoretically, by reaching back in the extended family to a previous generation, it might be possible to find such a person and utilize a multiple generation approach to the therapy. The parents of hospitalized children and adolescents with emotional illness are frequently involved in the therapeutic process. It is a rarity for grandparents to be brought in, and it is also rare for the parents of a hospitalized adult to be involved in therapeutic efforts. Realistically, however, involvement of several generations of the family does not work even where the hospital staff makes the attempt to do so. There are a number of reasons for this failure. Often, members of the previous generation may not be available; when they are available, they may be emotionally distant and disinterested. Some parents resent being bothered with the troubles of their adult children. If interested, members of the previous generation may lack the base of power needed in order to be effective in the system. Unless they have the leverage of power, aged persons rarely can exert the leverage required to promote change.

The "family with the schizophrenic member" differs from the "schizoprenic family" in that in the former, there appears to be a higher level of functioning by other family members. There may be high levels of social or vocational achievement; on an emotional level, however, significant members possess low levels of self. They function with what Bowen has described as "pseudo-self" rather than solid self. Because these families appear to be functioning better, therapists are often fooled into expecting a great deal of effort by these families directed at working on change. The effort that they make is, for the most part, on a verbal level. On an action level, little happens. These are the families who are quite cooperative while the identified patient is hospitalized; but, when the patient is discharged they fail to continue in treatment.

A third variety of family, one whose characteristics lie somewhere between those of the "schizophrenic family" and the "family of the schizophrenic," is the family that produces a drug abuser. Members of these families suffer from an impoverishment of self. This impoverishment is transmitted from generation to generation in much the same manner as are the characteristics of families residing in the slums. They have developed an alienated lifestyle. The individuals are cut off from each other and from their families of origin. This type of family system creates "no self" individuals who lack the ability to differentiate. These families rarely see their part in the problem and engage in only a surface participation in therapy (Entin and Schumann, 1971). Generally speaking, this type of family should be treated with a more structured approach than is possible with the Bowen Theory.

The Bowen Theory, with its requirement of differentiation of feeling and thinking systems, is, after all, a cognitive approach to therapy. To expect persons whose primary symptomatology focuses on disordered thinking to respond to cognitive techniques can, in itself, be indicative of disordered thinking.

Perhaps, the type of hospitalized patient most amenable to the Bowen Theory therapy is the one with an affective disorder. These patients and their families generally function at a higher level of differentiation than either of the schizophrenic varieties. Although depressed patients will suffer diminished self-esteem, they have a more intact self than those functioning at the schizophrenic level. There is also a concomitantly higher level of self in other family members. In general, depressed patients and their families have a greater level of cognitive functioning than do the schizophrenics.

In a 1977 article, I discuss a method of using family therapy in the treatment of the depressed patient while working solely with the patient. Bowen theory can also be effective while working with the patient and spouse or patient and family. Durkheim (1951) recognized the importance of the family relationship in depression nearly a century ago. In a study of suicide, he postulated that the greater the density of the family, the greater the immunity of the individual to suicide; and, the less integrated the individual to society and family life, the greater the risk. In other words, the more one is involved in a satisfying meaningful relationship within the family system, the greater the immunity from depressive states.

Family therapy of the depressed patient involves aiding the patient to accomplish a higher level of self-esteem and to achieve a person-to-person relationship on an adult level with the significant components of the family system. If the patient has been cut off either by feelings or by actual distance from one or both parents, he is encouraged to break through the cut-off. If a parent is no longer living, he is encouraged to work toward resolving the destructive feelings in the relationship which impede his ability to achieve a higher level of self-esteem. The following example is illustrative of this type of approach.

> Connie, a woman in her early twenties, returned to live in the same community with her parents following her divorce. She had been the child who was most involved in the parental emotional system while growing up. Whenever her parents

suffered financial setbacks or physical illnesses, she would take it upon herself to try to make things better for them. She worked hard at being a good daughter.

Each parent suffered from a variety of chronic, physical illnesses. She too, developed a psychosomatic illness. Each person in the family triangle expected succor and support from the other. The parents, an emotionally skewed couple, provided each other with some of the support needed but expected Connie to supply the remainder. When this was not forthcoming, they would play the "you don't love me, you are bad" game. Connie, seeking solace for her own pains, received little empathic return; instead she found additional pain in her relationship with them. She began to be a bad daughter, a hopeless, unworthy human being. These thoughts then culminated in a suicide attempt.

Therapy consisted of occasional sessions with all three members of the family, sessions with the parents together, with Connie alone, and with the mother alone. Although there were three people involved, there was not one complete self.

It became apparent in the early sessions that the parents were so emotionally intertwined with each other that any attempt to put change in that relationship would be extremely difficult, and perhaps destructive to each. Efforts, therefore, were focused on aiding Connie in developing a higher level of self, independent of the parental emotional system. This consisted of helping her to realize that she was not responsible for her parents and their feelings, and that she did not need to continue in the role of "parent" to them.

Although the extreme tightness of the parental relationship made it difficult for her to establish a separate person-to-person relationship with each, she became able to deal with them as a unit without feeling outnumbered. In this way, she was able to maintain a workable relationship with them without suffering the loss of her own self and without having to cut off from them. In the process she was able to establish a new self concept that in turn helped her to achieve a more satisfying independent social life and a higher level of accomplishment in her profession.

Connie's ability to differentiate from her parents was made easier because the expectation that society has of children is that they move away from their parents in adulthood. In a situation where a marital partner is fertilizing the pathology of the spouse, societal expectation works the opposite way. Closeness, support, sharing and caring are the expectations, and often this results in a worsening rather than an amelioration of the pathology. It is essential when this occurs that the spouse be assisted to achieve a high enough level of differentiation so that he or she is no longer feeding into the pathology.

> Harry was a 31-year-old male with a history of psychosomatic complaints resulting in this assumption that he is disabled. He has made a number of suicide attempts. His wife, a member of one of the helping professions, developed an intense concern for his well-being throughout the years of their marriage. Her existence became devoted to lightening his "burden." His excessive demands for physical comfort, some of which were quite bizarre, fostered an underlying resentment, which also served to heighten her protective activity.
>
> In the family sessions, she came to realize that the more she did for him the greater his demands, and she began to change the way she reacted to him. As is predictable in a system, when she changed, he tried to return the relationship to its former level. His effort was in the form of a highly dramatic and nearly successful suicide attempt. Instead of reacting in her previous manner, she was able to maintain her "I" position. As she began to demonstrate less responsiblity for him, he slowly began to accept a more responsible role for himself.

Each of the above illustrations deals with a family system in which there is an identified patient. In one, the focus of therapy was on that person, in the other, therapy of the system was primarily directed at the one not designated as patient. In each, the focus of therapy was directed at the healthiest component of the system; the one who possessed enough self to be able to change self and, thus, bring about change in the functioning of the entire system.

Summary

The Bowen Theory, although originally developed as a treatment modality for hospitalized schizophrenics and their families, has not proven to be effective for that purpose. Efficacy has been impeded by a number of factors, the most significant of which are the: inherent nature of the hospital system wherein the focus of treatment has been historically on the individual; operational characteristics of families in viewing the problem as residing solely in the symptomatic member; low level of differentiation of self generally found in members of schizophrenic families; and basic cognitive roots of the Bowen Theory which make it, for the most part, incompatible with disordered thinking.

On the other hand, the Bowen Theory has been efficacious when utilized in the treatment of patients with affective disorders. In the families of these patients, there is generally found to be at least one person who functions at a high enough level of differentiation as to be able to change the way the family system functions.

References

Bowen, M. The family as the unit of study and treatment. *American Journal of Orthopsychiatry,* 1961, *31,* 40-60.

Bowen, M. The use of family therapy in clinical practice. *Comprehensive Psychiatry,* 1966, *7,* 345-374.

Bowen, M. Videotape lectures. Medical College of Virginia, Richmond, VA. 1968.

Bowen, M. Theory in the practice of psychotherapy. In P. Guerin (Ed.), *Family therapy: Theory and practice.* N.Y.: Gardner Press, 1976.

Bowen, M. The use of family therapy in clinical practice. *Family therapy in clinical practice.* N.Y.: Jason Aronson, 1978a.

Bowen, M. Family therapy after twenty years. *Family therapy in clinical practice.* N.Y.: Jason Aronson, 1978b.

Bowen, M. An interview with Murray Bowen. *Family therapy in clinical practice.* N.Y.: Jason Aronson, 1978c.

Durkheim, E. *Suicide.* New York: The Free Press, 1951.

Entin, A. & Schumann, M. An exploratory study of the families of drug using adolescents. In J. Bradt & C. Moynihan (Eds.), *Systems Therapy.* Washington, D.C., 1971.

Framo, J. Cronicle of a struggle to establish a family unit within a community health center. In P. Guerin (Ed.). *Family Therapy.* New York: Gardner Press, 1976.

GAP Report No. 78: The field of family therapy. Group for the Advancement of Psychiatry. New York: 1970.

Lidz, T. *The origin and treatment of schizophrenic disorders.* London: Hutchinson & Co., 1973.

Luber, R. Teaching models in marital therapy: A review and research issue. *Behavior Modification,* 1978, *2,* 77-91.

O'Leary, D. & Turkewitz, H. Marital therapy from a behavioral perspective. In T. Paolino & B. McCrady (Eds.), *Marriage and marital therapy.* N.Y.: Brunner/Mazel, 1978.

Schumann, M. The depressive component in family systems. In J. Lorio & L. McCleaathan (Eds.), *Georgetown family symposia: Vol 2.* Washington, D.C.: Georgetown University Family Center, 1977.

Weiss, R. The conceptualization of marriage from a behavioral perspective. In T. Paolino & B. McCrady (Eds.), *Marriage and marital therapy.* N.Y.: Brunner/Mazel, 1978.

Chapter 3

RELATIONSHIP ENHANCEMENT THERAPY WITH INPATIENTS AND THEIR FAMILIES

Edward Vogelsong
Bernard G. Guerney, Jr.
Louise F. Guerney

EDITOR'S COMMENTS

In recent years, the function of communication in the family, and more specifically communication in the marital relationship and its role in marital satisfaction, has received a great deal of attention. In 1973 the American Psychiatric Association reported that communications problems were evident in 85 percent of those marriages considered to be dysfunctional (Luber, 1978). Rose (1977), however, points out:

> Despite this consensus on the critical role of communication processes, it has yet to be demonstrated whether communications difficulties are the cause or result of relationship problems. It does appear, however, that a strong relationship between measures of communications effectiveness and marital satisfaction does exist (p. 231).

Given this empirical indication a number of treatment approaches have been developed which focus specifically on dyadic or family communications processes and techniques. In general these approaches have several common characteristics including the following:

- The techniques are basically behavioral in orientation although some forms have a Rogerian or "empathic understanding" theoretical basis (Carkhuff, 1969);
- Most forms are short-term, structured and didactic or educational in approach;
- Modeling, shaping, role-playing, practice and feedback are the generally accepted and most frequently utilized treatment procedures;
- Often, communications techniques are combined with other procedures (most frequently, problem solving training or contingency contracting) to form a "treatment package" approach to marital dysfunction;
- Several of these approaches have been the object of empirical investigation and initial findings suggest the efficacy of the model in producing positive changes in the areas of communication effectiveness and marital satisfaction (Luber, 1978).

It should also be noted that in most cases communications training techniques have initially been developed as interventions for marital or dyadic relationship dysfunctions. They would fit into the scheme Olson (1975) describes as a "quasi-interactional system" the primary therapeutic goal of which is to systematically change and improve the interactional style of the dyad. In most cases, the dyad either involves the marital couple or a parent and child. Very little literature is available, even of a descriptive nature, delineating the application of communications techniques with entire family units.

Because communications models of treatment have a basic dyadic tradition, it is worth noting a disagreement which currently exists in the field regarding the classification of marital therapy in general. On the one hand, the authors of the following chapter consider family therapy to be any intervention which attempts to alter the family system regardless of the number of individuals involved (Chapter 3, note 1). On the other hand, Whitaker (1975) states:

I define marital therapy as *the treatment of a couple who have no children*. . . . Treatment of the husband-wife axis within a two-generation unit, that is, treatment of the parents without their children, is probably better defined as family therapy of a subgroup. . . . Actually, psychotherapy of the husband-wife axis, is really just one inefficient method of treating this subgroup as the family scapegoat, just as we used to mistakenly treat the child member because of the symptoms he or she had in defense of the whole family (p. 166).

Regardless of this theoretical controversy, the fact remains that communications models are among the most popular and thoroughly researched approaches in the field today. In attempting to define their relationship to other family therapy approaches, however, communications skills training is probably better classified as a *therapy* than as a *theory*. Thus, as a treatment technique, this approach can be incorporated into a variety of diverse theoretical frameworks. It is, of course, most closely associated with the behavioral orientation; it is also an important element in the newly developing marital and family "enrichment" programs. These attempt to provide growth-producing experiences in situations which are basically sound but where a desire for even more satisfying relationships is expressed (Gurman and Kniskern, 1978). Again, as stated above, communications skills training approaches are frequently utilized in conjunction with other treatment techniques to form a "treatment package" intervention.

Given the well developed models of this treatment and the encouraging empirical support for its efficacy, it seems that communications training should be an important intervention for all therapists regardless of theoretical orientation. It provides a firm base upon which to build a comprehensive family treatment plan.

The following chapter describes one comprehensive skills approach called Relationship Enhancement. The authors describe the techniques in detail as well as delineating various applications with the hospitalized patient and his/her family; in addition, group and multiple family group formats are considered.

Raymond F. Luber

Introduction
Relationship Enhancement

Therapeutic intervention designed to teach family members how to enhance relationships between a member who is hospitalized and other members of the family can contribute to the successful treatment of the patient in the hospital and can create a different interpersonal climate. It can result in a more favorable prognosis when the patient is discharged.

With inpatients and their families, the Relationship Enhancement (RE) method seeks to change the characteristic patterns of interpersonal interactions by teaching one or more members of the family network skills that permit them to establish more harmonious and satisfying interactions. The objective is to create an enduring, facilitative, interpersonal climate for positive ego development. Where vicious cycles destructive to the patients' development exist, RE therapy attempts to encourage communications which will help to build self-esteem and self-confidence. RE seeks to replace interactions which create conflict and uncertainty in patients about the behaviors necessary to fulfill their own and other's emotional needs, with attitudes and actions designed to promote self-understanding and greater acceptance of others. Where conscious and unconscious deceptions predominate, RE seeks to promote open, direct communications and actions.

In this chapter, we present a brief overview of RE therapy methods and describe their use with psychiatric patients and their families.

Relationship Enhancement Therapy

In RE therapy, the improvement of interpersonal harmony and personal development is brought about by means of teaching specific skills. Participants are taught to express themselves in constructive ways and to minimize the arousal of defensiveness and hostility in others. Participants practice acknowledging the subjectivity of their views, rather than making value judgments or analyzing each other's motives. They are taught to express underlying, positive feelings.

All the skills taught in the program are intended to act in concert to enhance intimacy and emotional gratification and to prevent discussion from degenerating into unproductive digressions or accusations and counter-accusations. These skills focus the discussion on more fundamental aspects of the relationship and its problems. Therefore, they facilitate problem resolution.

In accord with social learning and reinforcement principles, the skills are taught through systematic leader demonstration and exemplification and by participants practicing skills under intensive and extensive supervision and appropriate reinforcement by the therapist. Participants receive individual instruction from the leader, and, if working in a group, they strengthen their learning by teaching others while they themselves are learning. Concrete suggestions are provided for daily practice and maintenance of the skills in the natural environment. Skills to promote generalization are taught and practiced.

RE is an effective technique for dealing with both *interpersonal* and *intrapersonal* difficulties. Intrapersonal gains are achieved through RE skills when one family member is able to help another gain fuller understanding and awareness. The use of symbionts (persons whose actions are inherently significant to each other's adjustment, with family members a prime example) as effective therapeutic agents for one another, has been discussed more fully elsewhere (B. G. Guerney, 1969).

Specifically, all participants are taught six sets of behavioral skills or modes of behavior. Explanation of the skills, as they are described to clients, may be found elsewhere (B. G. Guerney, 1977).

Expresser Mode

The Expresser mode is designed to increase the participants' awareness of their own feelings, perceptions, and desires as they pertain to important interpersonal relationships. Participants are taught to communicate this awareness in a way that will increase the possibility of being understood and responded to in a compassionate way. In RE therapy, both patients and symbionts are encouraged to look not only at the immediate incident which led to an episode of frustration, anger, disappointment, and the like, but to long-standing patterns that they wish to improve and establish. They are taught to look not just at the negative but also the positive aspects of their relationships. By means of Expresser skills, participants can clearly communicate the attitudes and behaviors of others which serve as blocks or impediments to achieving satisfaction and growth, and they can clearly delineate those behaviors which would serve to provide an enriching relationship.

During RE training, the Expresser mode is used any time a person is initiating a discussion or reacting to what another has said. Whenever an opinion, a point of view, a thought, or a feeling is expressed, the person who is speaking is the Expresser and is obligated to follow the guidelines for the Expresser mode. A total of six guidelines are taught for functioning in the Expresser mode. For all presentations of guidelines in this paper, dyadic interactions are assumed, since in RE, most commonly the Expresser directs comments to a selected individual.

The first guideline helps the second person to be more receptive to the speaker's message. It prepares the other to listen more carefully to the Expresser. The Expresser accomplishes this by acknowledging the needs, attitudes, and feelings of the other person before expressing his or her own needs, attitudes, and feelings.

The second guideline requires that views be stated subjectively rather than citing them as objective, morally valid, or normatively correct. This guideline is designed to reduce to a minimum the other's defensiveness and to minimize any need to dispute the Expresser's views.

The third guideline urges the Expresser to present any feelings that have any bearing on the issues under discussion. It is explained that such expression will enable the relevant parties to understand behaviors rising from those feelings.

The fourth guideline further prepares the other party to be more compassionate and understanding than ordinarily would be the case. It does so by requiring the Expresser, when he or she is voicing a complaint, and when it is emotionally and intellectually possible to do so, to search for and to express hidden positive feelings toward the other person which often underlie the feelings.

The fifth guideline is designed to prevent dialogues from taking off on flights of exaggeration, mutual recrimination, and name-calling, which otherwise could cause the discussion to degenerate. This guideline requires the Expresser to be specific and descriptive of actual events and behaviors in describing what is upsetting about the other's behavior.

The last guideline urges the Expresser to seek a solution by presenting an "interpersonal message." An interpersonal message is a request for new, more satisfying, attitudes and behaviors from others. It includes a statement of the anticipated positive reactions. Clients are also urged never to forget that interpersonal messages may be used to go not only from the negative to the positive, but also from the positive to the extraordinary. (An example would be a couple communicating about improving already satisfactory sexual interactions).

Empathic Responder Mode

While one person is in the Expresser mode, another person is designated to listen and demonstrate understanding. This person is called the Empathic Responder. The role of the Empathic Responder is to create an environment in which the Expresser feels accepted and worthwhile as a person. This is accomplished by: a. focusing attention on the essential content and the emotions of the Expresser in order to reach the deepest possible level of compassionate understanding, including the implications the statement has for the relationship (the implicit interpersonal message); and b. communicating this understanding and compassion to the other party by word and manner, thus, further facilitating openness from the Expresser. The exchange can be about an interpersonal issue between the Expresser and Responder, or it can be the exploration of an intrapersonal concern of the Expresser's.

The RE therapist, in instructing the Empathic Responder mode, must be careful to emphasize the need to recognize and state the positive feelings of the Expresser as well as negative ones. The implicit positive feelings and attitudes are less obvious, but very important for nurturing positive relationships. For example, an Expresser complaining about lack of attention usually is implicitly expressing the view that the other person basically is held in very high esteem or affection, which is the reason the attention is wanted. This should be recognized in the empathic response. Finally, the participants are made aware, as frequently as necessary, that empathic responses do not imply agreement, but acceptance; the Empathic Responder may have different perceptions which can be expressed when in the Expresser mode. Thus, each party has an opportunity to verbalize fully without challenge and to learn how to be receptive and respectful of the other's perceptions. The assurance of equity in understanding and acceptance, provided and carefully monitored by the therapist until participants learn to operate within the guidelines independently, reduces communication conflict and increases trusting attitudes.

Mode Switching

Both empathic and expressive skills are useful to help another work through an emotional problem of his or her own, or to resolve an interpersonal problem between two or more parties engaged in a dialogue. In either usage, certain superordinal skills are necessary to bring the issue to a successful resolution. These skills are labeled Mode-Switching skills. The guidelines used here give the participants the ability to keep in mind which of the above modes of behavior is being employed at any give time; the ability to know when to employ one mode and when the other; and how to move from one mode to another in a way that is coordinated with the other person.

Problem-Solving and Conflict Resolution Skills

When problems stem from disagreement on a set of values or on an appropriate course of behavior, the Expresser and Empathic Responder modes help to clarify the issues and often result, by themselves, in problem/conflict resolution. When problems require very specific decisions and agreements, however, another set of RE skills is brought into play: Problem/Conflict Resolution Skills—all used while they continue to use Expresser, Empathic Responder, and Mode-Switching skills. The problem-solving skills assure that the participants:

- Set aside a suitable amount of time in an appropriate place to consider problems jointly and separately.
- Take the necessary steps to assure themselves, before they press for solution, that they fully understand both the emotional and interpersonal aspects of the problem.
- Seek solutions that are aimed at increasing *mutual* need satisfactions.
- Propose, receive, and react cognitively to the proposed solution of the other with a high degree of operational clarity and react affectively in a way that will further encourage careful and fair problem solving.
- Attempt to foresee the consequences and difficulties of any suggested solution in order to permit careful and realistic refinements at the outset.
- Make plans for a systematic reassessment of agreements reached in order to make revisions as may later be found necessary.

Facilitator Mode

Once participants have become adept at functioning in a set of skills, they are fully instructed in how to facilitate the use of these skills by others. In the Facilitator mode, participants learn how to help each other in the therapy session as well as in the course of everyday living. Even if a family member has not attended the therapy sessions previously, a Facilitator can gradually and gently help that person become more expressive and learn how to empathize better.

Maintaining and Generalizing Skills

The goal of RE is to help family members use the skills they have learned in the therapy sessions in their everyday lives. Once they begin to demonstrate skill proficiency in the home sessions, they are asked to practice and use the skills at home. If family members have been trained as facilitators, the process is considerably easier. At home, families are asked to set aside short periods of time for practice, for example, 30 minutes weekly. They begin with topics that are easy to discuss. As the therapy continues and skill levels increase, family members are asked to spend longer or more frequent times practicing at home to discuss more difficult issues. Gradually, the therapy session is used to supervise the home practice sessions. In this way, the family becomes less dependent on the therapist and more capable of handling its own problems constructively.

Therapist's Role

The therapist serves as an instructor in RE. The therapist's role is to teach family members the RE skills, motivate them to see their value for relationships and personal adjustment, and to make the entire process exciting and rewarding. It also is part of the therapist's task to encourage generalizaton so that patients and their families, now and in the future, use the skills to resolve problems, and promote psychological growth.

The therapist always serves as a model for family members by conveying the same understanding, acceptance, and concern that they are learning to express to each other. The therapist, however, never provides empathy or support when it can, instead, be provided by another family member. The therapist carefully reinforces family members for each new step toward mastery of the skills. The therapist gently reminds them when they are not following the guidelines and suggests appropriate skillful reformulations.

Historical Background

Although the designation, Relationship Enhancement, was not used at the time, development of RE therapy began with Filial therapy in 1962 (Guerney, 1964). That was the first program in which nonprofessionals were instructed systematically in the rationale, attitudes, and skills used by professional psychotherapists for purposes of helping them to help an intimate—in that case, their child—toward improved mental health. Research (Guerney and Stover, 1971; Guerney, 1976) and clinical experience showed Filial therapy to be very effective. Most parents of emotionally disturbed children were able to apply therapeutic skills at home, both in special play sessions and in their daily interactions.

More important, from the point of view of this discussion, parents trained to use therapeutic skills with their children reported these skills to be beneficial in improving relationships with older children and with friends, colleagues, and spouses. These reports supported our view (Guerney, 1969) that family members could be effective therapeutic agents for one another.

Eventually, this gave rise to therapy formats for families and subgroups of families, such as fathers and sons (Ginsberg, 1977), and mothers and daughters (Vogelsong, 1975; Coufal, 1975).

In family RE (Guerney, 1977), the entire family (or a group comprised of two small families) is trained together. As in other family approaches, it is preferable to work with all members of a family unit. RE family therapy, however, can also be employed when one member of a marital couple (or member(s) of a larger family) will not (or cannot) participate, through the extensive use of role-playing by the therapist of missing family members. (Note 1).

In those sessions with a significant person absent, the therapist fills in for the missing person or persons by role-playing their parts during skills practice. By taking role cues from what is known about the family, the therapist thus prepares the participants for more constructive family interactions. The intention, as may forthrightly be explained to participants, is to allow family members and patients to elicit from significant others those kinds of responses which are most conducive to their satisfaction and growth. It is also designed to avoid making statements which are likely to incite counterproductive responses from others.

Research

A large number of RE studies have been conducted (all in outpatient or training settings). Waiting-list, no-treatment groups, and alternative treatment control groups have been employed; in some studies, subjects have been randomly assigned to comparison treatment conditions. Measures used in RE research have included behavioral as well as self-report instruments, and in one study an unobtrusive measure was included. Low socioeconomic and educational groups as well as middle class groups have been studied. The variables measured have included both the mastery of the specific skills and more general variables, such as communication patterns, problem solving, trust, harmony, relationship satisfaction, and self-concept.

The results of the research have been reported in detail elsewhere (Coufal, 1975; Guerney, 1977; Vogelsong, 1975). Therefore, we will provide only a brief overview here. Positive results have been found on all of the types of variables mentioned above. Whenever they were studied, follow-up gains for RE participants were found; in one such study, the superiority of RE over a traditionally oriented discussion method was evident not only at termination, but also six months later. Such superiority in comparison with another widely used method would appear to rule out alternative explanations such as attention, placebo, suggestion, and "thank-you" effects. Finally, the results indicate that low socioeconomic and educational status do not prohibit clients from making significant gains in RE.

The extent to which the same conclusions can be valid for inpatients depends on the degree to which inpatients and their families respond differently to RE methods than the populations studied previously. Research directed toward answering that question, despite the difficulty in implementation and interpretation, would be very valuable. Inpatients are comprised of many different subgroups, each of which might require separate consideration. To date, clinical experience does not suggest that there need be any fundamental changes in the nature of RE therapy for inpatients and their families.

Using RE with Psychiatric Patients and Their Families

RE therapy is a flexible intervention approach that can be used in a variety of ways for treating psychiatric patients and their families. In some instances, it is possible to work with patients and family members together. At other times, family members can meet with the therapists to learn RE skills they can use with the patient only during visits and after the patient has returned home. In the hospital setting, RE also can be used with patients as a form of group therapy. In these groups, patients learn RE skills which they apply to their families. To the extent that patients are willing and able, they should be included in the family RE sessions whenever feasible.

Working with the Patient and Family Together

Family visits to the patient in a psychiatric hospital are frequently traumatic and sometimes lead to regression in the patient's behavior. For the patient, a visit from the family can be a reminder of some of the old, painful patterns of behavior and the social stigma of being hospitalized. For the families, the visit can be associated with the stigma, since it is a reminder that one of their members has been hospitalized and can bring an awareness that they might have contributed to the pathology. It is also depressing for many families to visit the patients because the patients frequently reject them or treat them in inappropriate ways.

RE can provide an effective alternative to these unconstructive contacts if it is conducted in conjunction with family visits. The social visits can be either replaced or supplemented by a structured session in which all family members systematically learn and practice RE skills. Even when the patient is not capable of participating in an active way, there are advantages to having the family meet with the patient and learn RE skills. If the patient is receptive to the words family members use, it will be encouraging to hear communication proceeding in constructive ways. If the patient is not receptive to the words, there may still be some impact from the various moods that are conveyed and the warmth that is expressed toward the patient. Family members who previously believed there was nothing they could do to help the patient, soon begin to realize that they can interact in ways that will convey their concern and care. By including the patient in these skills-learning sessions, the family members indicate their interest in working together in whatever ways are possible and desirable.

When RE is conducted in the hospital, the frequency and length of sessions are determined by the ability of the family to visit the patient and the length of time the patient is capable of meeting with them. Weekly sessions are desirable if possible. Although there are some advantages to having extended sessions of three to four hours, it is unrealistic to expect many patients to be able to participate for that length of time. It is possible, however, for the therapist to meet with family members for an extended period of time and have the patient join them for only a portion of the session. This arrangement would be particularly appropriate when family members can visit only occasionally. In such sessions, the therapist first explains the skills and then demonstrates them in conversation with each family member individually. The therapist then becomes the Expresser and engages in a separate dialogue with each. In this way, everyone has a brief opportunity to practice Empathic Responder skills. Family members then begin practicing with each other, first with non-threatening topics, and as their skills improve, with important issues in their relationships. Throughout the entire process, the therapist remains neutral regarding subject matter that is expressed. The therapist's attention is focused entirely on helping family members learn the skills and use them in their exchanges with each other. The therapist's attitude is always one of warmth, reinforcement, encouragement, and support.

By proceeding in this structured and systematic way, family discussions are channeled into constructive methods for dealing with issues and resolving problems. The therapist sets realistic expectations for each participant so that at the end of each session all family members can be reinforced for what they have learned. The satisfaction gained from having previously challenging or argumentative family members now understanding some troublesome feelings serves to encourage family members to continue with RE.

Working with the Family without the Patient

Although it is most desirable to have all family members present while practicing empathic and open communication, there are circumstances when that is not feasible. For example, when family members feel so hostile that they cannot even temporarily relate constructively to a patient, it would be counterproductive for the family members and the patient to meet. More likely, the determination of the patient's inclusion in the groups is a function of a number of patient variables. Generally speaking, to the extent that the patient's incapacities prevent participation in the process, it is necessary to use a format in which other members of the family take the major responsibility as change agents for the patient as well as themselves. Variables which must be considered in determining a patient's incapacities for inclusion are the qualities of: reality contact, control of self, and cooperation. If the status of the patients on these dimensions are such that they would be disruptive to the learning of others without acquiring skills themselves, they should not be included. Reaction to medication would be another relevant variable, drowsiness, for example, would be a serious deterrent to learning.

When family members take the major responsibility for initiating change, it is unreasonable to expect immediate reciprocal changes. Nevertheless, assuming sufficient reality contact, different responses eventually may be pulled from the patient which will be more positive, and, thus, start a cycle of more constructive interaction. Eventually, the patient may be incorporated into the RE learning process.

When family members learn to use RE skills with someone who is not present in the family sessions, the absent family member is role-played by someone who is present. Thus, they are provided the opportunity to learn and practice the various modes in a way that closely simulates actual family exchanges. Initially, the therapist may wish to demonstrate the role-playing techniques by playing the patient, and in so doing provide each family member with an opportunity to respond to patient behaviors using the skills approach. Later, as family members become more comfortable, they may take turns imitating the absent person. The role player should act as much as possible like the patient and not use RE skills. In this way, the family has an opportunity to deal with troublesome patient behaviors in a supervised non-threatening way. Once family members have become proficient in using RE skills in response to role-played patient behaviors, they are encouraged to begin using the skills in whatever contact they have with the patient. They then report their experiences to the therapist, discuss problems they have had, and proceed to work on more difficult issues. Family members are always cautioned to start using skills with the patient in situations of low risk so that they are likely to experience success. Once they have gained confidence and are experienced, they can begin to use the skills in more difficult situations.

During such sessions, the emphasis is on skill training, not on an analysis of the patient's illness. Discussion of the patient's symptoms is appropriate only when it will clarify the role play so that family members can gain practice in responding to particular behaviors.

It is not required that sessions without the hospitalized patient be devoted entirely to the patient. In fact, when they have bearing or an effect on the relationship with the patient, it is desirable that the other family members concern themselves with relationships among themselves and their inner problems and conflicts. In reality, the therapist generally does not need to force this on the family members. Being responded to empathically generally makes them want to disclose their own troublesome feelings and interpersonal problems.

Multiple Family Formats

Multiple family formats may be employed in either community or hospital settings. These would be of particular value where only one family member beyond the hospitalized patient is involved. A viable group can be formed of, for example, spouses or a mixture of spouses and two or three family members of a larger family. A typical group includes between six and eight members. In this format, the patients can also be included full- or part-time. Both family members and patients can benefit from the multiple family format for the usual reasons that group therapy is valuable. In such groups, however, patients would need to be cooperative because non-cooperation would require extensive use of the therapist's time, thus, making it impossible for the therapist to give adequate attention to the increased number of participants. The same point would hold if other family members were uncooperative. Lack of cooperation is not the primary reason for avoiding the multiple family format; it is the time of the therapist in relation to numbers that is the critical issue. As a matter of fact, an uncooperative family placed with a cooperative one can make greater strides than when seen alone because of peer modeling and desire to adhere to norms.

Again, if patients (or other family members) were absent from a multiple family group, the therapist would assume the major responsibility for role playing the missing members. In order to permit the family members to see empathic responses modeled in the face of provocative behaviors, the therapist, at times, plays the role of a family member who is present, while the latter role plays the patient.

One such group was conducted for married people whose spouses were hospitalized. Two patients were in psychiatric units while the others were hospitalized for major surgery, physical rehabilitation, and long-term illness. All of the group members had contact with their hospitalized spouses at least once a month. All reported that the use of RE skills helped them achieve a closer relationship with their spouses. A case example follows for one of the group members.

> Sue was especially encouraged by the RE training. Her husband, Harold, had been hospitalized several times since his return from Vietnam. During these times he had become withdrawn, depressed, and occasionally hallucinated. In the past, Sue had always told him to forget about what was bothering him; it was past and he need not worry about it any longer. She had tried to cheer him up by talking about their children, the garden, and other things. When Sue learned RE skills, she encouraged her husband to talk with her about what was bothering him instead of trying to distract and cheer him up. Her empathic responses facilitated Harold's talking about the many frightening experiences he had had in the war. He sobbed as he related his guilt and fear to Sue; he has been afraid that she would reject him for what he had done. Instead, he was overwhelmed by her acceptance. Sue reported she had never realized what Harold had been through. Now she understood him better and was able to talk with him about his fears. They felt much closer to each other. Harold is now employed in the community and has not been hospitalized for several years.

Working with Families in a Non-hospital Setting

There are practical issues as well as attitudinal ones that sometimes make it difficult to work with the family in the hospital setting regardless of what the family's level of motivation might be. Distance to be traveled, lack of time, or scheduling problems in working with the family can make a community setting more appropriate. This type of arrangement can be made from the outset of the patient's hospitalization, or it can be started later, prior to the time when the patient would be returning for home visits, or, if all else fails, before the patient is to be discharged from the hospital to the community. Home visits can be used as an opportunity for family members to interact with skills in relation to the patient, having been trained prior to the patient's return. It is also possible to include the patient in family RE sessions in these home visits, which can be a constructive way for family members to spend the time home with the patient. Patients have less fear of returning home when they can see the family using more constructive patterns of interaction.

After the patient is discharged from the hospital, families should continue in RE sessions with the patient participating. This procedure is essential to help the patient maintain gains and prevent the family from falling back into ways that are destructive to the patient.

Training non-hospitalized family members in a community facility has some advantages because community personnel frequently are more available than hospital personnel for undertaking therapy. Working with a single family is easier, and multiple family arrangements are usually more easily arranged when visiting hours and long distances do not have to be considered. For multiple family formats, it is not necessary that all participants be related to a psychiatric patient. Families work only on relationships within their respective families during the RE sessions. They interact only by facilitating each other in the learning and practicing of RE skills. Homogeneity of type of problems faced is helpful, but generally is not of major importance.

Working with the Inpatient, but not the Family

Just as families can be taught skills for use with the absent hospitalized member, inpatients can be taught RE skills independent of the family for use with their families and other significant people in their lives. There are several ways that RE can be used with patients in a hospital setting.

In small groups, patients meet together to learn and practice RE skills (Note 2). In addition to creating a warm, supporting climate, the therapist provides instruction in the various RE modes, being careful to pace progress to ensure success. Because the skills training is highly structured, the therapist is able to control diversions, confrontations, and personal attacks which frequently occur in some other types of group therapy. The expectation that patients will listen to the Expresser and attempt to respond empathically (with the therapist serving as a model of these behaviors) tends to promote constructive exchanges.

Patients first practice the skills with the therapist and then with each other. For most patients, it is a new and positive experience to be able to relate to others in this way. The empathy and acceptance which they extend to each other (with the encouragement and reinforcement of the therapist) permits such groups to develop into deeply meaningful support experiences for the members.

Inpatient RE groups can be open or closed groups. Anyone is welcome to join. The patients can participate as frequently as they wish. Generally, groups meet daily (or at least several times a week) for between 60 and 90 minutes. Since the subjects to be discussed are determined by the Expresser at each session and responded to ahistorically, there is no history that members are required to have in order to relate helpfully to other members of the group.

Patients should not be required to participate in RE sessions. Those who choose not to participate, however, can be encouraged to sit in on a session to observe what the program is like. Such patients should be permitted to take the next step when they wish; there is no explicit or implicit suggestion that full participation will soon be expected. This acceptance not only of expression, but of non-expression—unconditional acceptance for the patient—can be facilitative in its own right.

Even patients who choose to join often will not participate actively at the beginning. In RE therapy, the degree of self-disclosure and amount of activity are at the discretion of the participant. Thus, patients can maintain their own level of comfort regarding participation and content. Even when patients choose to sit and observe others interacting, they may gain insight and improve their perceptions of reality.

When patients are able to use the skills with others in the group in an appropriate way, they are encouraged to use them with staff and other patients on the ward outside of the group. Frequently, a kind of game develops between patients and staff in which they use Responder skills to restate almost everything another person says. These kinds of interactions are encouraged because they give patients practice in responding in new ways to everyday situations and help them to work through their uneasiness in using RE skills. Such games are recognized as steps in the right direction and are reinforced by the active involvement of others in the games and by actual praise.

However awkward their use of the skills might be, it must be remembered that even the *attempt* to use the Empathic Mode is likely to reduce negative, inappropriate, and idiosyncratic communications and increase accurate awareness of others in the environment.

In order to give patients practice in using the skills with their families, role plays are conducted in the group therapy meetings. First, the therapist role plays family members of the patients. Later, patients may be asked to role play their respective family members.

After patients have become proficient through this role playing and confident and comfortable about their use of the skills, they are encouraged to use RE skills when visiting with their families. It is especially important to guide them toward using the skills in low-risk situations only. After some success, they may begin to apply the skills to some of the more difficult problem areas. After each visit with the family, the patients discuss their experiences with the therapist and the group and work out difficulties they have encountered in the use of the skills. Here again, the therapist reinforces every effort the patient has made and provides encouragement for continuing to use RE skills with family members.

If family members have learned the skills independently, either in the hospital or in a community setting, the ease with which the patient can employ the skills will be increased. If the training has been separate, a visit at the hospital or at home can include a session with a RE therapist who will supervise the efforts families make in applying the skills with the patient present and vice versa. The presence of the therapist, while family members and patient are interacting in modes for the first time, will facilitate application in this more demanding context. (Since all RE therapists follow the same structured model, previous contact between this at-home therapist and the family, although helpful because of trust and rapport factors, is not absolutely necessary).

> Anna provides a typical example of how a patient can benefit from learning RE skills. For all 21 years of her life, Anna lived with her parents. Her grades in high school were below average. After she graduated, she had a hard time keeping a job. She developed strong dependency relationships with several boyfriends, who subsequently dropped her. On several occasions, Anna made superficial cuts on her wrists and was taken to the emergency room of the hospital. After Anna took a mild overdose of sleeping pills, Anna's doctor recommended that she be hospitalized in a local community mental health center inpatient unit. Anna agreed to the admission. She joined

a RE group that met every afternoon for an hour on the ward. In the group, Anna expressed feelings of worthlessness about herself and her fear of being rejected by her current boyfriend. She expressed anger toward her parents for not giving her the same love and attention that she perceived they had given her younger sister, who was now in college. During Anna's hospitalization, the therapist met several times with Anna's parents and taught them RE skills without Anna being present. When Anna was discharged, the therapist met every week with Anna and her parents together. The parents were surprised to learn of Anna' feelings of rejection by them. They indicated that they loved her a great deal and were concerned about her, but did not know what to do. Her attempted suicides had been very frightening to them. Anna was surprised at the depth of her parents' feelings and was gratified to learn of their love. After Anna and her parents were able to label the positive interpersonal messages they had previously not identified in their relationship, it was easier for them to work out ways of relating to each other more effectively. Anna's parents learned how to give her the attention she needed, and the love they felt for her, without forcing her to act out to get it. For the last nine months, Anna has had a steady job, and she is now looking for an apartment to share with a girlfriend.

Summary

In RE therapy, family members are taught skills which enable them to express greater understanding, awareness, sensitivity, honesty, compassions, and openness toward each other. These skills are taught in a highly-structured, systematic way. The therapist provides instruction, demonstration, modeling, social reinforcement, encouragement, and prompting to teach the skills. Homework is provided and participants are taught ways to steadily increase their use of the skills at home.

Even when families are separated by the hospitalization of one member, there are a variety of ways that RE can be used as a family intervention program. When it is possible for families to meet regularly with the hospitalized patient, and the patient is capable of participating in an active or passive way that is not counterproductive to family interactions or the patient's progress, it is desirable to conduct RE therapy with all family members present. When it is not possible for the family to meet together, RE can be used with family members in the absence of the patient to teach skills that can be used to improve relationships with the patient during visits, or when the patient is back at home.

RE can also be taught to patients in the hospital setting, either individually or in small groups. In these therapy groups, patients first apply RE skills to their relationships with each other and with hospital personnel. Patients and family members can be taught RE skills independently in this way, and later brought together to apply these skills to their relationships with each other. If skills training must be limited during hospitalization to only the family or only the patient, the family relationships can still be improved, since use of the skills by any member of a family unit can have impact on the entire family. Also, instruction in RE includes teaching participants to teach others the skills, and to encourage others to use them. Regardless of the format that has been used, it is highly desirable to arrange for RE sessions to be conducted with the entire family after the patient has been discharged in order to increase transfer and generalization and maintain facilitative skill levels.

Notes

1. We concur with Olson's (1970) definition of family therapy as "any therapeutic intervention which has as its focus the alteration of the family system. From this perspective, it is not a prerequisite of family therapy that more than a single individual be involved" (p. 514).
2. For patients who are missing even the most elementary interactional skills, some preliminary training is recommended in basic social skills acquisition (Authier, 1973; Goldstein, 1973).

References

Authier, J. *A STEP group therapy program based on levels of interpersonal communication*. Unpublished manuscript, University of Nebraska College of Medicine, 1973.

Carkhuff, R.R. *Helping and human relations* (2 vols.). New York: Holt, Rinehart and Winston, 1969.

Coufal, J.D. *Preventive-therapeutic programs for mothers and adolescent daughters: Skill training versus discussion methods*. Unpublished doctoral dissertation, The Pennsylvania State University, 1975.

Ginsberg, B.G. Parent-adolescent relationship development program. In B.G. Guerney, Jr., (Ed.). *Relationship enhancement: Skill-training programs for therapy, problem prevention, and enrichment*. San Francisco: Jossey-Bass, 1977.

Goldstein, A. *Structured learning therapy*. New York: Academic Press, 1973.

Guerney, B.G., Jr. Filial therapy: Description and rationale. *Journal of Consulting Psychology,* 1964, *28*(4), 303-310.

Guerney, B.G., Jr. (Ed.). *Psychotherapeutic agents: New roles for nonprofessionals, parents, and teachers.* New York: Holt, Rinehart and Winston, 1969.

Guerney, B.G., Jr. Filial therapy used as a treatment method for disturbed children. *Evaluation,* 1976, *3,* 34-35.

Guerney, B.G., Jr. (Ed.). *Relationship enhancement: Skill training programs for therapy, problem prevention, and enrichment.* San Francisco: Jossey-Bass, 1977.

Guerney, B.G., Jr., & Stover, L. *Filial therapy: Final report on MH 1826401.* Unpublished manuscript, 1971. (Available from The Pennsylvania State University, Individual and Family Consultation Center, Catherine Beecher House, University Park, Pa. 16802).

Gurman, A., & Kniskern, D. Research on marital and family therapy: Progress, perspective, and prospect. In S. Garfield & A. Bergen (Eds.), *Handbook of psychotherapy and behavior change: An Empirical Analysis.* (2nd Ed.). Chickester: John Wiley & Sons. 1978.

Luber, R. Teaching models in marital therapy: A review and research issue. *Behavior Modification,* 1978, *2,* 77-92.

Olson, D.H. Marital and family therapy: Integrative review and critique. *Journal of Marriage and the Family,* 1970, *32,* 501-538.

Olson, D.H. Marital and family therapy: A clinical overview. In A.S. Gurman & D.G. Rice (Eds.), *Couples in conflict.* N.Y.: Jason Aronson, 1975.

Rose, S. Communications skills workshop. *Group therapy: A behavioral approach.* Englewood Cliffs, N.J.: Prentice-Hall, Inc., 1977.

Vogelsong, E.L. *Preventive-therapeutic programs for mothers and adolescent daughters: A follow-up of relationship enhancement versus discussion and booster versus no-booster methods.* Unpublished doctoral dissertation, The Pennsylvania State University, 1975.

Whitaker, C.A. A family therapist looks at marital therapy. In A.S. Gurman & D.G. Rice (Eds.), *Couples in conflict.* NY: Jason Aronson, 1975.

Chapter 4

BEHAVIOR MODIFICATION
APPROACHES

Eugenie Wheeler

EDITOR'S COMMENTS

As mentioned in the editorial comments to Chapter 2, it is only in recent years that behaviorists have entered the field of family therapy, and this entry has been largely determined (some might say inhibited) by the basic learning theory orientation of traditional behavior modification approaches. Quite naturally, therefore, techniques for achieving specific behavioral changes in individuals have been the mainstays of behavior marital/family therapy.

Indeed, the "deviant" or "maladaptive" individual has traditionally been the target of behavioral intervention; this is also essentially true in the area of family therapy. As a matter of fact, behaviorists rarely utilize the term "family therapy" although they have been quite active in the conceptualization of marriage and the treatment of marital discord (Liberman, 1970; Weiss, 1978). Also, behavioral therapists have generally been primarily concerned with families in which there is a specific, identifiable problem such as alcoholism, sexual dysfunction, or delinquency. In addition, they have shown primary concern for intervention with intact or traditional families and settings (Mash, Hamerlynck and Handy, 1976).

As has been described by Mash et al., (1976), family therapy from the behavioral perspective has focused on methods by which parents are able to control or modify the behavior of children; Mash, et al. states, "The involvement of the family has typically been in terms of providing a context for the occurrence and subsequent modification of the child's behavior" (p.XV). In addition, considerable effort has been exerted in the area of childrearing methods.

Several criticisms have been directed toward the behavioral approach. For example, Bowen contends that although this treatment will, indeed, produce short-term changes, lasting effects will not be achieved because behavioral therapists do not attempt to modify the emotional level of the individual. It is of interest to note that at least a portion of this criticism appears to be supported by research evidence. That is, a significant number of studies indicate treatment deterioration "on criteria most central to and valued by behavior therapists" (Gurman & Kniskern, 1978, p. 856).

Another broad area of criticism is concerned with the tendency of the behavioral approach to consistently regard the child as the "deviant" family member and to adopt the overriding goal of "retraining" the child. As Gurman and Kniskern (1978) point out, this represents a significantly different perspective from that of most non-behavioral family therapists who would view the child's "deviant" behavior as *functional* for the family system rather than merely reflecting the parents' deficits in cognitive learning skills. Indeed, many non-behavioral therapists would contend that the family system is often invested in the "deviant child" *not* changing. In general, it appears that in the area of marital and family therapy, the behaviorists have developed several important techniques for the modification of overt, observable behaviors in individual family members, most especially the "deviant child." They have, however, been reluctant to broaden their perspective to view the family in any thoroughly systemic manner; this, of course, is consistent with the social learning presuppositions of the behavioral orientation.

Finally, several characteristics common to the behavioral approach to family therapy should be indicated, including the use of interventions which are generally educationally oriented, aimed at specific problematic behaviors and are designed to be relatively short term. In addition, behavioral therapists strongly emphasize the utilization of those techniques which are supported by empirical evidence and can be evaluated in terms of their efficacy.

The following chapter describes in detail the theoretical basis of behavioral family therapy, specific intervention techniques and their application to family treatment.

Raymond F. Luber

Introduction

Behavior Modification is based on learning theory. Symptoms are viewed as learned maladaptive behaviors and behavioral therapy is viewed as a teaching-learning process. Behavior Modification is systematic. It is based on a growing body of research and operates on the assumption that behavior is influenced by its environmental antecedents and by the responses it evokes from significant others in the individual's environment. Behavioral therapists operate on the premise that if behavior changes, it elicits different consequences, and if new behaviors are sufficiently reinforced and rewarded, they will be incorporated into the client's pattern of responding.

In behavior therapy, one focuses attention on behavior. It is believed that when behavior changes, changes in feelings follow. More traditional approaches tend to start with feelings in the hope that when they can be changed, changes in behavior will follow. This process can be a lengthy one. Behavior therapy is usually short term and is always goal-oriented.

When using a behavioral approach to psychotherapy, psychiatric problems are put into behavioral terms. The first step is to identify the problem. The therapist listens carefully to the client's concerns, his/her reasons for wanting help, and then together, the therapist and client work toward defining the problem in specific, concrete, observable, behavioral terms. One convenient means of organizing a patient's behavior in such terms is to decide which behaviors are excessive (undesirable, maladaptive) and which are lacking (desirable, adaptive). Behaviorists differentiate between talking about anxiety and the concomitants of anxiety such as trembling, sweating, muscular tension or headaches. For example, if every time Burt works late, his wife Gwen, develops a headache or reaches for a martini, which in turn results in Burt's working longer hours, the behavioral analyst would describe the interaction between the client's behavior (resorting to physical symptoms—drinking) and the environment, especially the interpersonal or human environment, in this case her husband's absence from the home. This leads to insights about what environmental factors are maintaining problem behavior or preventing the emergence of adaptive behavior. This is a very specific way of doing what therapists call study, diagnosis and treatment. It is the method by which the problem is operationally defined.

Family and marital therapy provide an excellent opportunity for the use of behavioral techniques. The major reinforcers in an individual's life space are members of the family with whom interaction occurs every day (Liberman, 1972). In recent years, behaviorally oriented therapists have begun working with families to maximize the chances for meaningful and enduring behavior modification. If the problem is depression, for example, the therapist attacks the depression by helping the patient make behavioral changes in order to increase the level of positive reinforcement received from his/her significant others. The task is to identify where there has been a drop in reinforcement so that intervention can be geared to gaining more gratification for the client from the environment. Family interaction can be modified to ensure more reinforcement for appropriate activity and less for depressive behavior, such as withdrawal.

Goals

In behavioral marriage counseling, the first step is to translate the problem into behavioral terms. If one of the partners is asking for more compassion or understanding the therapist will ask him/her to specify how he/she wants the partner to express compassion or understanding. Is he/she requesting more verbal behaviors, such as solicitous questions, offers to listen, or offers of help? More affection, or sexual responsiveness may be the request. Or the individual may need more specific help with the children and chores. Clarification of goals is the first step in developing a treatment program. Therapists call this "starting where the patient is." Helping the patient to define where he/she is and wants may be the only way to reach well formulated, mutually understood goals.

Targeting the problem behavior to be changed (increased, decreased or introduced) is the first step toward the formulation of goals. Goals, too, must be specific. "To feel better" or even "to learn to be more assertive" are too vague to be useful. Goals should describe specific behaviors the client wishes to accomplish in performance terms as well as the conditions under which this is to occur.

Treatment Program

A sound treatment program, in addition to clearly stated goals includes: Reinforcement or built-in rewards to provide for sustained motivation, counseling strategies or interventions to be used to implement the program, and methods of evaluating the program in terms of the goals.

Reinforcement

In the behavior modification theory, a reinforcer is not defined by its intrinsic properties, by subjective feelings, or by cultural stereotypes. A stimulus or an activity becomes a reinforcer when it actually results in increases in the strength, intensity, or frequency of the behavior which it follows. The reinforcement may be extrinsic initially, such as praise from the therapist, parent, or a classroom teacher. Other concrete extrinsic reinforcements can be tokens, gold stars, or use of the family car. In successful therapy, extrinsic reinforcement will then be replaced by intrinsic reinforcement such as the joy of a job well done or the pleasure of learning, or the satisfaction of enhanced marital communication.

Part of the effectiveness of this approach hinges on finding out exactly what is reinforcing to each particular client. Assumptions about the meaning of money, praise, food, or free time, can be erroneous and must be determined carefully. In family therapy, parents can often confuse a reward with a bribe. A bribe is payment for a corrupt or immoral act while reinforcement is feedback that works to increase any behavior. Behavior therapists recognize that the therapist is usually a powerful reinforcer to the patient.

Counseling Strategies

Effective behavior change methods include shaping, token economies, contingency contracting, instigation therapy (homework assignments), assertiveness training, systematic desensitization, and anxiety management training. These strategies may be used in various combinations. They are effective for use with individuals, couples, families, and groups. These behavior modification techniques are used in inpatient, day-treatment, and outpatient settings. After describing these techniques, their application with patients in psychiatric settings will be discussed.

Shaping

One of the most important behavioral principles for clinical application is that of "shaping" behavior. Shaping is working gradually toward a specific goal by reinforcing successive steps leading to the goal. This method is also called conditioning by successive approximation and is used to develop desirable behaviors that are not already in the patient's repertoire. The shaping process involves reinforcement of selected responses which proceed in the desired direction and the non-reinforcement of those that do not. For example, if the goal is to reinstate a behavior such as helping with household chores and the children have not been doing these chores for the duration of the mother's hospitalization, the therapist cannot wait for them to set the table or empty the trash before issuing reinforcement. Instead, the children must be rewarded for the slightest approximation toward keeping the house running smoothly. Shaping is, thus, particularly useful in situations where desired response rarely, if ever, occurs or when the parents or therapist do not wish to wait for the behavior to occur. The therapist must teach the parents to reinforce the older children for putting things away, helping the younger siblings put away their toys, and reinforcing them when they perform these tasks. Some teachers and parents are skilled at shaping behavior almost intuitively. They are able to reward successive approximations leading to such behaviors as putting on coats and boots, or completing classroom assignments. Parents can be taught to reinforce steps toward completing homework instead of waiting until the end-of-the-year report cards when it is often too late. Truants need to be reinforced for small periods of time during which they remain in school, rather than having praise withheld until the questionable goal of perfect attendance is reached.

Another example of shaping involves a therapist helping parents and children find creative ways to reinforce grandmother, who is recovering from a stroke, so she will practice the skills she has to relearn whether such skills involve speech, walking, or use of her hands. The family members can learn to recognize the importance of starting where the patient is and celebrate small successes instead of expecting too much progress at one time. Skills cannot be learned, or relearned, all at once; shaping provides for appropriately graduated steps. The therapist's task is to move at the patient's pace with clearly set goals and to see that reinforcement is offered for successive approximations to the final desired behavior goal.

Shaping occurred in therapy with a woman, Emily, and her teen-age daughter, Roberta, who had a destructive relationship. The therapist first reinforced Emily for allowing Roberta more privacy. He praised Emily when she discontinued the practice of reading Roberta's diary, and allowed Roberta more hours away from home. He reinforced Roberta when she modified some of her rude verbal behavior (stopped calling her mother names) and when she shared with Emily some of the responsibility for baby-sitting and errands. The goal was to teach them, over time, to reinforce each other for the behavior they wanted from each other so that the relationship could become less mutually hostile and more mutually supportive. The father's role was assessed and he facilitated the process by becoming involved in shaping Emily's behavior from over protectiveness and manipulation toward more direct communication; he also aided in changing Roberta's behavior from destructive rebellion to more responsible and satisfying behavior.

In these examples, the behavioral progress is maintained by the natural reinforcers (family) around the patient. An important step in any behavior therapy procedure is the final one of carrying over treatment effects from the hospital or clinic to the natural environment.

As in all other behavioral approaches, one way is to find out what is reinforcing to the particular patient, whether it be toys, money, clothes, hugs, or verbal praise and then to give these reinforcers at the appropriate times in the appropriate amounts to keep the process moving. Although this approach has something in common with supportive therapy, the major difference is in the specificity and the goal-orientation of behavior modification.

Token Economies

A token economy is the use of tangible reinforcement when social reinforcement is insufficient. Tokens can be points, play money, or anything that represents or can be exchanged for things or privileges that the client wants. Token economies are used in institutions to modify patient behavior, but the concept can be adapted to any setting. The token economy is a microcosm of society outside the institution. The therapeutic environment is structured to show the direct relationships between work and reward, striving, and success. It is particularly effective with the apathetic, institutionalized patient. Patients can earn tokens for a variety of actions to help them attain more adaptive modes of living, and programs can be individualized to meet their particular needs. Tokens can be earned by cooperation in housekeeping routines, occupational therapy, grooming, or manners. The importance of rewarding small increments of improved behavior, or shaping, applies to token economies as well.

The system begins with a list of target behaviors or goals which are considered constructive and functional. Goals might include: becoming active on a ward committee, taking prescribed medicine, giving feedback in group therapy, or attending occupational therapy. Rewards and privileges, which the patient values, are then specified. Rewards can be tangible items such as food or coffee, activities such as outings, or social reinforcement such as praise from the therapist.

> Judy and her therapist targeted as behaviors to be changed, getting out of bed on time for breakfast, making friends with another patient, writing to members of her family and responding to them appropriately when they visited. She received a previously specified number of tokens for each step toward each accomplishment. She saved up these tokens to "buy" certain privileges. The family cooperated in establishing the privileges

as items of clothing (tangible), and a home visit to include a shopping spree (activity). As she gradually assumed more responsibility for her behavior, she received more praise and encouragement from the staff. In time, this generalized improvement in her behavior at home resulted in more positive family interaction which had been the ultimate goal. The intermediate step of using the token economy as a strategy of intervention was necessary to establish more functional and goal-oriented behavior. At the same time, work was done with the family to help them modify their pattern of reaction to the patient's behavior.

Contingency Contracting

Contracting is a behavioral treatment technique used to make each of the elements of the process so explicit that they can be written into an agreement for behavioral change that is understandable and acceptable to all involved. DeRisi and Butz (1977) indicate that "contracting is a method of insuring that each party to the agreement—husband, wife, child, social worker, delinquent, teacher, probation officer—obtains an acceptable number of those rewards (including behavior change) that please him." From the clinician's standpoint, contracting is both a goal and a method. It is a goal because a new contract is the end result, the permanent product of each treatment session. It is also a method for reaching the other goals of treatment. The contracting process can defuse potentially explosive situations and shift the focus from hostile blame to problem-solving.

As in shaping and token economies, the process starts with the targeting of a behavior to be changed. This must be described in behavioral terms so the behavior can be observed; then, reinforcers must be selected in order to provide sustained motivation. The next step is to locate the appropriate people who are able to monitor the behavior and issue the reinforcers. It is not until all of these steps have been accomplished that the actual contract is written. The contract must be understood and agreed upon by all persons involved. Implementation consists of data collection, trouble shooting where necessary, continued monitoring and re-writing until each behavior shows improvement and the goals are achieved.

Contracting depends on negotiation. There is no such thing as imposing a contract since that is a contradiction in terms. In behavioral contracting, each party has the freedom to determine terms and conditions without coercion. Alleged abuses of behavioral methods, as in prisons, are frequently based on approaches described as "behavior modification" in the generic sense without reference to this well-defined process of psychological counseling.

Contingency contracting is a recent and promising approach to solving many human problems partly because it allows for a systematic monitoring that improves accountability by accurately measuring progress.

A marital contract might have items such as:

Gwen's Privileges
Bert's Responsibilities
When Gwen visits home from the hospital, Bert will go to church with her and the children.

Bert will visit Gwen at the hospital a minimum of twice this month.

Gwen's Responsibilities
Bert's Privileges
Gwen will show appreciation to Bert's mother for her caring for the children during Gwen's hospitalization by thanking her in writing or in person by the end of this month.

Gwen will write a letter to the children once a week for positive statements about her activities.

Another example is:

Paula had made a suicide attempt after an altercation with her adolescent son, Bob, and the termination of a relationship with a boyfriend. She was hospitalized for six days. Part of the contract developed during discharge planning to implement the problem-solving process included the following items:

Bob's Privileges
Paula's Responsibilities
Will attend a course in Parent Effectiveness.

Will increase social contacts with friends by planning a social activity for at least two evenings a week.

Will allow Bob to have friends at home and be polite to them.

Will cook Bob's favorite meal at least once a week.

Will not be critical of Bob's friends.

Paula's Privileges
Bob's Responsibilities
Will attend school regularly, will be home by 8:00 p.m. week nights and midnight on Saturday nights unless previous arrangements have been made.

Will be polite to Mother's friends, male and female.

Will have dinner with Mother and sisters at least three nights a week.

Will not call Mother "crazy."

Instigation Therapy

"Instigation therapy" is another term for homework. All good therapists recognize that not enough can happen in one or two hours a week to bring about significant change. What happens during the other 167 hours is important, too. Behavior therapists put great emphasis on planned, structured assignments as an integral part of the therapeutic process.

Attending group therapy, keeping a list of "self-put downs" for use in group therapy, initiating a conversation with a staff member, making a request of a family member regarding more letters or visits, participating in some form of exercise, and discussing a particular point in the next family therapy session or during the next home visit are all examples of structured assignments. For the aged patient, life review techniques can be adapted as assignments leading to linkages between generations and increased grandparent/grandchild communication.

Assertiveness Training

In assertiveness training the therapist teaches patients more effective social interaction through modeling, prompting, role-playing and positive feedback, or reinforcement. It is based on the theory that passivity or aggressiveness in social relations leads to anxiety, depression, and frustration. The "happy medium" is assertiveness which involves fulfilling one's needs and rights without violating anyone else's rights, putting anyone else down or allowing one's own rights to be violated. Patients are taught to express their feelings in direct, honest ways but without accusations or hostility. Central to the method is involving patients in "role-playing" scenes where the participants rehearse incidents in relationships they wish to improve. Sometimes, a hierarchy of scenes is developed involving ascending levels of emotional threat and learning difficulty. Only when a patient satisfactorily carries out a situation in "real life" does he/she move to the next step up in the hierarchy. Effective performance in the therapy group is rated on the basis of the content, fluency, and conciseness of the conversation, as well as on the tone of voice, facial expression, physical gestures, and eye contact; all of these are concrete behaviors. Other participants in the group model the scene, illustrating that there is more than one effective way to express feelings, and that there is a vast range of choices on the behavioral continuum from passive to aggressive. The learning of these options diminishes the participants' feelings of helplessness and anxiety and increases their confidence and effectiveness.

> Tilly had been hospitalized for several months before she was able to make use of an assertiveness training group. Her hierarchy involved approaching her husband assertively during his visits about issues she had not been able to address constructively before. Her responses to his demands had swung from martyrdom and withdrawal to the other extreme, violence. She practiced discussing use of the family car, budget, in-law problems, and child management, in that order, and in reasonable

terms. When she approached her husband in a new way, he responded with more attention and reasonableness than she had anticipated and their interaction improved.

Systematic Desensitization

Systematic desensitization is a counter-conditioning technique used to help individuals reduce anxiety reactions; it is especially effective with phobias and is comprised of several steps. First, the anxiety-provoking situations are identified, and then ordered according to the level of anxiety which is aroused. Then, relaxation procedures are taught. After the patient is relaxed, he/she is asked to imagine the anxiety-provoking situations sequentially. When his/her relaxation gives away to tension, the procedure is repeated until the patient can tolerate the feared situation in real life while trying to remain relaxed.

There are variations in this process; sometimes role-playing scenes are more appropriate than imaginary scenes. This can result in a combination of assertiveness training and desensitization. (Wolpe, Brady, Serber, Agras, Liberman, 1973).

> Clarisse had a problem of sexual dysfunction that was seriously jeopardizing her relationship with her husband. Desensitization as a supplement to sexual counseling was the treatment of choice. As her own anxiety diminished and she was able to be more relaxed, she was able to enjoy and communicate sexual feelings. As Clarisse and her husband were able to communicate better on all levels, their enjoyment of each other's company increased. This had a positive impact on the entire family; a ripple effect resulted so that other problems in the area of child management began to diminish. The parents were so enthusiastic about the results of desensitization that they brought their son to the clinic for similar treatment for pre-test anxiety.

Anxiety Management Training (AMT)

Anxiety management training is a variant of systematic desensitization in which patients are taught to use the awareness of their own physical symptoms of anxiety as stimuli for relaxation (Suinn and Richardson, 1971). Since it is impossible to be relaxed and anxious at the same time, this is an effective method of diminishing anxiety. To help patients sustain relaxation, they are encouraged to visualize a serene scene—a graphic, imagined setting that represents peace and tranquility. The switching of scenes is practiced from anxiety sensations to relaxation, from anxiety sensations to imagery of tranquility, and from sensations of anxiety to imagined scenes of competence and mastery. To be able to relax or picture a serene scene in the face of anxiety gives one a feeling of mastery. To learn to "turn it on" at will, patients are asked to visualize an anxiety scene (a situation that makes them feel tense and insecure). They are asked to be aware of their own subjective, physical concomitants of anxiety in upsetting situations so that eventually the physical feelings themselves will act as a stimulus for relaxation and thoughts of serenity and mastery. The switching of scenes is a constructive use of imagery for promoting anxiety management.

> Martha's scene was being with her family and having all of her grandchildren around her, asleep. Her limited tolerance for noise and confusion had interfered with her having satisfying relationships with these children. She became so tense and anxious at the thought of taking any responsibility for them that she could only be around the children for very short periods of time. With an intensive treatment program focused on Anxiety Management Training, she became less anxious in their presence and learned ways to lower her anxiety level in the face of many family situations that she could not handle before her treatment.
>
> Joan's serene scene was being in bed with the covers pulled up over her head. Her anxiety scene involved her daughter coming home from school stoned. As she was able to gain a feeling of being more in control of her moods, she was able to deal with her daughter less hysterically and more effectively. A combination of A.M.T. and assertive training made it possible for her to deal with her older children, also, without impulsive, hostile outbursts, uncontrollable anxiety and guilt. As Joan was more in control of, and less victimized by her moods, she became a better listener and the other members of her family had less resistance to be around her. After a short period of group A.M.T., she chose to change her serene scene to an outdoor setting; she also had a more difficult time getting in touch with her initial anxiety scene.

Setting

For behavioral family treatment to be successful in the psychiatric setting, there must be generalization of the results when the patient returns to home and community. Generalization is a term derived from learning theory and used by behavior therapists to evaluate the spread and durability of treatment effects (Liberman, McCann and Wallace, 1976). In behavior modification approaches to family intervention with psychiatric patients, the key element in promoting generalization is involvement of the patient's family throughout the therapeutic process. The importance of bridging the gap from hospital to home cannot be overemphasized because the alternative is repeated hospitalization. Transfer of learning or adaptation of newly acquired skills to new settings can best be achieved by making creative use of the hospital setting while working with the patient and his/her family during the period of hospitalization and planning for continued generalization after discharge.

Requirements

A hospital setting may seem antithetical to an approach that is based on an educational rather than on a medical model. Behavioral approaches to family therapy, however, can be practiced in any setting, including psychiatric hospitals, as long as behavioral assessments can be made, deficits identified, and appropriate contingencies and reinforcements brought to bear. The effectiveness of the approach is more dependent on therapist variables than on treatment variables.

For treatment to work, there has to be official sanction. Without administrative backing and clear role definition, clinicians may have to spend a disproportionate amount of time interpreting their function. It is also important that the staff be flexible, cooperative, and willing to try new approaches. If staff members working with the therapist are mature, and have a stronger focus on outcome than on process, then there is a viable environment in which to work.

The behavioral family therapist may have some concerns about working in a mental hospital and, of course, these would have to be considered before he/she could be in a position to help patients deal with their feelings about hospitalization. The greater the differences between therapist and patient, the more difficult it is to form a therapeutic alliance. If therapists do not have the skill and motivation to bridge these gaps with patients and their families, there cannot be mutual goal setting, skillful selection of individualized reinforcers, and the most humane treatment possible. This point has particular relevance to family intervention with hospitalized psychiatric patients because there cannot be the selectivity that is possible in other settings, especially in private practice. Intake cannot be controlled, difficult cases cannot be interspersed with high-functioning, easy-to-identify-with patients' families. Stigma felt by family members must also be considered. They may feel guilt and shame about having one of their members "put away," or dread visiting the hospital because of what it represents to them. These are all obstacles to the involvement of families in the treatment process and must be explored.

There can also be relatives who want to get rid of a "disturbing" individual and who are resistant to family therapy on that basis. Clinicians must always start with the relatives where they are, even if that literally means doing therapy in the home. Programs that involve more knowledge and understanding of the hospital or of the nature of mental illness can be helpful. In other situations, supportive groups of relatives, opportunities to ventilate, and relationship with a therapist can be useful in overcoming some of the obstacles to family involvement. The challenge is for the therapist to explore with staff and client what contingencies in this potentially averse environment can be arranged so that desirable behavior can be reinforced. Also, it is necessary to explore with family members what they are willing to contribute in time, interest, and other reinforcers.

The purpose or goals of treatment must be established and clarified to ensure that those of staff, patient, family, and therapist are not in conflict. Therapists concerned with the effectiveness of the services they provide, find that the behavioral approach to clinical problems has much to offer in the area of goal setting and evaluation. The emphasis on behavioral assessment (a method which helps the therapist to specify problems and goals in quantifiable terms) leads to specification and measurement. Data collection of objective and internal events is the underpinning of behavior therapy. This is inherited from a laboratory tradition. Treatment programs are evaluated in terms of previously determined goals at every step in the process, and the patient participates in the goal setting and the evaluation of the results of treatment to the extent that this is possible.

Current demands for accountability from public and private agencies make setting specific goals and evaluation of treatment important features. It is also ethically desirable to be able to document progress or its lack to both the therapist and to the client. Behavior modification provides the tools for this purpose and puts great emphasis on the importance of evaluation in terms of previously set goals.

The treatment goals in inpatient settings may be quite different from the goals in outpatient settings. Goldfarb (1971) states that the goal in institutional therapy may be to increase discharge rates, or minimize management problems, or perhaps to raise staff morale by changing patients' troublesome behavior. In outpatient settings the goals may be more related to decreasing depression and helping patients become integrated into the community.

Although allowances should be made for differences in settings due to the nature and degree of the patients' problems, basic therapeutic principles and goals do not change. Socialization, self-esteem, mobilization of resources, minimization of depression, and acquisition of behavioral skills are basic to all treatment situations. It is the level of treatment, rather than any differences in the theoretical underpinning, that would be considered significant to behaviorists.

The behavior to be shaped in the hospital might be extremely simple communication skills such as talking loud enough to be heard or increasing eye contact. In an outpatient psychiatric setting, the goal might be to achieve skills in applying for a job or requesting a spouse to become involved in marriage counseling. At all levels, a combination of strategies aimed at acquiring skills in communication would be the treatment of choice from a behavior modification point of view.

Time and Distance Constraints

The meaning of time in an institutional setting can be very different than in outpatient clinics. At least three aspects of the time use need to be considered, timing of the therapist/patient contact, timing of the therapist/family contact and timing of the contacts between the patient and members of his family.

Therapist/Patient Contact. Depending on the size of the caseload and other pressures, the therapist can usually capitalize on the availability of the patients' time—the fact that the patients are *there.* They, therefore, can be treated with more intensity, undiluted by broken appointments, waiting lists, and other delays. There is no dust-settling between appointments since they can be scheduled with appropriate frequency. This seemingly endless time span is a double-edged sword, however, because it can be difficult for patients to be time-oriented, or to relate to time structure in helpful ways. The suggestion that the patient participate in the process of setting appointment times can seem meaningless to the patient when he/she is there all the time anyway. The therapist must be more ingenious in discovering meaningful ways to involve the patient in planning for appointments, goal-setting, and in the entire treatment process.

With the trend toward briefer periods of hospitalization, there is a need for more effective short-term therapy with greater emphasis on generalization. Families need to be involved immediately in making the changes in the environment necessary to sustain changes in patient behavior. The hospital or day hospital setting needs to be as much like the home setting as possible so the carry-over of new behaviors from hospital to home can be facilitated. This transfer of learning is more apt to occur when the patient and family see the changes as newly acquired skills rather than as deep-seated personality changes.

Therapist/Family Contact. Family members often are not available for the necessary continuity in treatment. It is important for the therapist to be aware of the nature of the distancing whether it is primarily geographical, or whether the family member is distancing him/herself because of discomfort with the "identified patient" and all the feelings, including guilt, which the patient may arouse. Another area that probably needs to be explored is whether therapists themselves put up barriers because of some attitude, unconsciously and non-verbally communicated, to the effect that the family is no longer needed, that the "experts" are now taking over, or even that the family is to "blame" for the illness (in spite of common verbal assurances that the family's participation is more than welcome). In addition, therapists need to think more liberally about what constitutes "family," since assumptions about nuclear family units can distort what really composes the patient's significant social network. The "family" may be foster, adoptive, distantly related, neighborhood, or merely supportive friends; the helping staff members need to be open to seeing these networks so that potential support systems can be utilized for the benefit of the patient, regardless of their composition. If the family support is lost, therapists must expend a great deal of effort reconstructing a substitute support network for the patient as part of discharge planning.

Encouraging involvement on the part of the family can be extremely difficult; yet, without that involvement, generalization of patient gains will not be achieved since the patient returns to an unchanged environment. Some hospitals have developed successful programs of family therapy with relatives' participation in conjoint marital and family sessions. Classes and groups, including relatives, can be extremely helpful. Sometimes, these strategies only achieve the semblance of sound treatment, however. For example, the wife of a mental patient described how she went to a class in marital communication at the hospital so that she could take turns with the other wives standing watch and slipping into the lavatory to have sexual intercourse with her husband. The classes were almost meaningless to her because there was avoidance of any mention of sexual communication. Behavior modification programs are more realistically geared to the real goals of the patients and their families.

Patient/Family Contact. Fortunately, relationships do not depend entirely on the amount of time spent together, but, to a great extent, on the quality of the time spent together. This truism must be borne in mind by the therapist and taught to patients and their families. Otherwise, the constraints of time and distance can appear to be so overwhelming that motivation can be defeated and depression deepened. The following example illustrates this point:

> Beatrice understood the principle of positive reinforcement and was overextending herself to visit her boyfriend at the hospital regularly. The weekly 200-mile round trip was stressing to her physically, and gradually, her resentment was showing. Joe's response was fear and jealousy. The treatment of choice was assertive training for both. Beatrice learned to express her feelings more directly—that she loved him but her dread of the trip was having a bad effect on her. Joe felt reassured by her directness and since he was then less threatened, he was more open to a workable compromise. As a result of more assertive communication, Beatrice's trips became less frequent, but much more satisfying, and their visits were supplemented by more telephone communication. Both Joe and Beatrice reported that they felt less fearful that their relationship would deteriorate and more hopeful about their future, even though they were spending less actual time together.

In making the best use of the limited time that patients spend with their families, behavioral therapists often focus on recreation. This may seem surprising when there are so many immediate serious psychological problems to be treated. But, patients have so often lost their capacity to play and to enjoy time spent with family members that planning for recreation can help to shift the focus from problems to more positive pursuits. Brief, successful recreation can bring to light strengths, such as willingness to share or interest in acquiring skills, which aid in assessing potentials. Another reason for focusing on recreation is that communication in this area is less charged, threatened, and divisive. It is an area where children and other relatives can be more easily involved with positive results.

A combination of behavioral strategies needs to be brought to bear in working with families, as well as in working with patients. Hospitalization can serve as an opportunity to develop new recreational interests for later use with spouse and family. Occupational and recreational therapy can help toward generating positive mutual family participation when negative interaction has been the major mode of family interaction. Some therapists have persuaded marital partners to participate in relaxation therapy at the hospital and taught them how to continue it with the patient after he/she returned home.

Maximizing the Environment

An institutional setting has advantages because there is more control of the environment, yet this setting has disadvantages in terms of the variety and amount of reinforcers available. Much depends on the flexibility and imagination of the administration. Effective rewards such as privacy, freedom, use of personal clothing, or use of a telephone can run directly counter to administration policy. In outpatient settings, the thrust is more toward helping the client control the environment, since there is no hospital staff to do so. Examples of environmental control might be to plan for the individual to "Fat Proof" the home if weight loss is the goal. When child management is the concern, preparing a place for "time outs" and otherwise structuring the environment may be part of the plan. In institutions, the degree of control that the therapist exercises over the patient's environment should not be exaggerated. Large, regimented settings allow little room for individualizing patient needs. On the other hand, the degree of control should not be underestimated either, as expressions of support from staff members, therapist time, tokens, ground privileges, cigarettes, and certain responsibilities and recreational outlets can have a powerful positive impact. The possibilities of structuring the environment are more limited by the therapist's lack of imagination than by lack of potential reinforcers. Perhaps work in inpatient settings is more demanding creatively on the part of therapists. It is certainly more demanding of energy.

Chronically hospitalized psychotic patients often become docile, non-assertive, and apathetic in their hospital setting (Tucker, Perel, Wallace and Davis, 1976). They are at risk of losing their verbal skills if staff members are not present and actively facilitating verbal behavior. Group family therapy can be a helpful way to help patients "keep talking." Goldfarb (1971) states that in psychiatric settings, one purpose served by group therapy is the provision of real, immediate social satisfaction. Since the participants are apt to be more withdrawn than those in other settings, there is a need for more structure, direction and stimulation from the leaders. Behavior modification is more structured and more directive than most other therapies and is especially suited for inpatient use.

Co-leadership in group and family therapy is desirable in any setting for a variety of reasons including training and the provision of back-up in case of emergencies. In institutional settings, it is especially important to set a positive tone in therapy groups. If the interaction begins centering on the issue of who has made the most serious suicide attempts, the group can increase, rather than alleviate depression. Co-leaders can more easily get the group focused on how to improve coping methods and build self-esteem through modeling, warm-up exercises, and other innovative techniques. Therapists in institutional settings working with depressed patients may need to have a higher degree of energy and humor than therapists in other settings in order to be effective. Eckman and Liberman (1976) cite some advantages and disadvantages to treatment in a hospital setting.

On the positive side is the respite for the patient from involvement with others who may have encouraged the suicide attempts or other maladaptive behaviors, consciously or inadvertantly. There can be desirable aspects to the enforced pulling away from the toxic, familial interrelationships. This can be particularly true of brow-beaten women or anyone who is being cruelly treated. At the same time, to have the family living apart makes it impossible for the members to practice new ways of interacting on a day-to-day basis. The delay in reinforcement from significant others of newly acquired behavior is a real obstacle to treatment.

To overcome the obstacle of delay in institutional settings, reinforcement schedules can be useful tools. They are helpful to patients and therapists in identifying what is particularly reinforcing to a particular patient. Such a schedule can be developed to include the rewards available in the inpatient setting by the interdisciplinary team and by relatives. Reinforcers can include a wide range of categories from foods, home visits, attention from staff, helping with chores such as gardening or printing, serving on committees, taking courses, playing games, or field trips. They should be specific and the time lag between performance and reward as brief as possible.

It may be that the greatest challenge for family therapists in institutional settings is that of enlisting staff cooperation and support so that the family intervention is an integral part of the treatment program. This may be especially true for behavioral therapists because reinforcement schedules must be consistent and there may need to be considerable counting of behaviors, monitoring of contracts and issuing of rewards. Token economies have proven to be effective, especially in institutional settings but they are dependent on a high degree of staff cooperation. Consequently, the behavior therapy model requires a whole separate set of skills, including demonstrating its worth to colleagues, teaching it to technicians, and enlisting staff participation. This requires not only selling/teaching skills, but a high degree of dedication, energy and enthusiasm.

Sometimes, the principles of positive reinforcement can be applied with so much skill and creativity that the benefits of brief visits from families and correspondence are maximized, hope is sustained, and behavioral change is achieved. Planning for visits in the immediate future and projects on release can often facilitate treatment. Concrete rewards such as gifts, movies, and treats can be another factor; in addition new patterns of communication involving more encouragement and fewer put-downs can all be steps toward helping patients and families use family therapy in institutional settings. The behavioral therapist works to use these reinforcers as contingencies, spurs to growth, and a means to change behavior. The chronicity of the patient may be so discouraging to relatives that work with them must focus on the recognition of tiny increments of change and ways to consequate them.

As for successful outcome, setting step-wise and limited goals is a major feature (Liberman, McCann and Wallace, 1976). Working with families to maintain consistency in reinforcement contingencies from hospital to community, using natural reinforcers, pinpointing functional behaviors as therapeutic goals, and family therapy as a part of after-care programming are methods that promote generalization.

Summary

Feelings cannot be changed directly, but behavior can, and feelings are directly affected by behavior. With this knowledge, the therapist and patient, with the family, can structure the patient's environment, whether institutional or community, to elicit the kind of responses that will in turn stimulate him/her to do things that will bring more gratification. There are many similarities between behavioral therapy and insight therapy in that the therapist and patient explore, together, how the patient has invited negative feedback from his environment. One example would be that the patient turns people off. But insight alone does not produce behavioral change. With proper reinforcement or support, the individual may be able to change his pattern of responding to people in such a way that he can invite more satisfying social interactions. Assertiveness training gives excellent testimony to how effective this approach to treatment can be.

Because behavior modification is based on learning theory, it follows that emotional crisis is interpreted as a breakdown in an individual's learned coping strategies. This concept distinguishes it from other therapies which assume that the cause stems from intrapsychic conflict. The selection of strategies to be used to implement a treatment program is based on a behavioral assessment, which is an identification of the deficits and excesses in the individual patient's behavior. Goals are formulated which involve the acquisition of skills. The learning may be constituted of an improvement in the patient's characteristic methods of coping with various stresses, or developing communication skills, or changing health habits. A treatment program may involve teaching the patient how to raise self-esteem by self-rewarding.

Some of the major techniques used in behavior modification have been summarized briefly. Justice cannot be done in such a brief space, even to the major strategies that were selected or to the many variations and combinations that are used effectively to change behavior.

This brief description is not comprehensive but is, rather, a survey of highlights. There is much in behavior therapy that can enhance the repertoire of skills of therapists regardless of their orientation. The focus is more problem centered than personality centered—a factor which partially accounts for its broad applicability, and for the fact that fewer alterations in technique are necessitated by the treatment setting. By acquiring skill in behavioral techniques, clinicians can learn a wide range of effective interventions which can be most rewarding to themselves and to their patients.

References

DeRisi, W. J., & Butz, G. *Writing behavioral contracts.* Champaign, IL: Research Press, 1977.

Eckman, T., & Liberman, R. P. Evaluation of a comprehensive treatment program for repeated sex offenders. Paper presented to the Annual Meeting of the American Psychological Association, Washington, D.C., 1976.

Goldfarb, A. Group therapy with the old and aged. *Comprehensive Group Therapy,* 1971.

Gurman, A. S., & Kniskern, D. P. Research on marital and family therapy: Progress perspective, and prospect. In S. Gargield & A. Bergis (Eds.), *Handbook of Psychotherapy and behavior change.* New York: John Wiley & Sons, 1978.

Hosford, R. E., & deVisser, L. A. J. M. *Behavioral approaches to counseling: An introduction.* Washington: American Personnel and Guidance Association, 1974.

Liberman, R. P. Behavioral approaches to family and couple therapy. *American Journal of Orthopsychiatry,* 1970, *40,* 106-118.

Liberman, R. P. *A guide to behavioral analysis and therapy.* Elmsford, N.Y.: Pergamon Press, 1972.

Liberman, R. P., Paul, R., King, L. W., DeRisi, W. J. and McCann, M. J. *Personal effectiveness: Guiding people to assert themselves and improve their social skills.* Champaign, IL: Research Press, 1975.

Liberman, R. P., McCann, M. J., & Wallace, C. Generalization of behavior therapy with psychotics. *British Journal of Psychiatry,* 1976, *129,* 490-496.

Liberman, R. P., DeRisl, W., & King, L. W. Behavioral Interventions with families. In J. Masserman (Ed.). *Current psychiatric therapies.* N.Y.: Grune & Stratton, 1973.

Mash, E. J., Hamerlynck, L. A., & Handy, L. C. Editors' Introduction. In E. J. Mash, L. A. Hamerlynck, & L. C. Handy (Eds.),·*Behavior modification and families.* New York: Brunner/Mazel, 1976.

Moss, G. R., & Liberman, R. P. Empericism in psychotherapy: Specification and measurement. *British Journal of Psychiatry,* 1975, *126,* 73-80.

Phelps, S., & Austin, N. *The assertive woman.* San Luis Obispo, CA: Impact Press, 1975.

Suinn, G. R., & Richardson, F. Anxiety management training: A nonspecific behavior therapy program for anxiety control. *Behavior Therapy,* 1971, *2,* 498-510.

Tucker, L., Perel, I., Wallace, C. J., & Davis, J. R. It's the stuff that keeps them talking. *Journal of Psychiatric Nursing and Mental Health Services,* 1976, *14,* 11-14.

Weiss, R. L. The conceptualization of marriage from a behavioral perspective. In. T. J. Paolino and B. S. McCrady (Eds.), *Marriage and marital therapy.* New York: Brunner/Mazel, 1978.

Wolpe, J. *The practice of behavior therapy.* N.Y.: Pergamon Press, 1974.

Wolpe, J., Brady, J. P., Serber, M., Agras, W. S., & Liberman, R. P. An overview of systematic desensitation. *American Journal of Psychiatry,* 1973, *130,* 961-965.

Chapter 5

THE STRUCTURAL APPROACH

Suzanne Goren

EDITOR'S COMMENTS

The structural approach to family therapy is exemplified in the works of Minuchin (1967, 1974, 1978). It focuses on the individual *within the context* of the family, rather than on the individual alone. Briefly, Minuchin (1974) delineates three basic axioms which form the foundation of structural family therapy:

- An individual's psychic life is not entirely an internal process; that is, the individual is influenced by and influences his environment.
- Changes in a family structure contribute to changes in the behavior and the inner psychic processes of the members of that system.
- When a therapist works with a patient or a patient family, his behavior becomes part of the context (p. 9).

According to structural theory, the family has specific properties and functions. It is an organized, self-perpetuating system which undergoes development and transformation and "adapts to changed circumstances so as to maintain continuity and enhance the psychosocial growth of each member" (p. 51). In addition, families have structure which organizes the interactions of its members. Two important structural elements of the family are subsystems and boundaries. Subsystems are the mechanisms by which families differentiate and execute their functions; boundaries, on the other hand, are the rules defining who participates in subsystems and how this participation is exercised. For proper functioning in the family, boundaries must be clearly defined.

A normal or adequately functioning family can be conceptualized as being multifaceted (Minuchin, 1974):

- A family is transformed over time, adapting and restructuring itself so as to continue functioning.
- The family has a structure which can be seen only in movement . . . the strength of the system depends on its ability to mobilize alternative transactional patterns when internal conditions of the family demand its restructuring.
- A family adapts to stress in a way that maintains family continuity while making restructuring possible (pp. 65-66).

Thus, as a social system in transition, even the normal family meets stress as it seeks to protect and socialize its members. At certain points, the family may need assitance in mobilizing its resources to accommodate new situations; such circumstances, however, may not be sufficient to permit a pathological label to be placed on the family. Rather, from the structural perspective, "the label of pathology would be reserved for families who, in the face of stress, increase the rigidity of their transactional patterns and boundaries, and avoid or resist any exploration of alternatives" (Minuchin, 1974, p. 60).

The structural therapist plays an active role in the treatment process by joining the family "with the goal of changing family organization in such a way that the family member's experiences change" (Minuchin, 1974, p. 13). Thus, intervention is aimed at the present and is directed toward the entire family system. Change is viewed as a process whereby the therapist aids in the restructuring of the family system to transform dysfunctional transactional patterns. The intervention is designed to usurp the dysfunctional operation of the system in order to facilitate a transformation in structure.

Like Bowen's approach, the structural orientation can be described as a "systems" method of family treatment. Despite this general alliance, there are distinct theoretical differences between the two methodologies. First, where Bowen actively supports working exclusively with family subsystems, such as the most "functional" or "motivated" family member, the structural orientation places major emphasis on treating the total system. As Minuchin states:

> Treatment of systems in which attention is paid to only one sub-
> system is frequent. But it is undesirable, uneconomical, and

sometimes ethically or humanly incorrect to ignore the other subsystem entirely (1974, p. 107).

Concretely, this distinction is also demonstrated in the basic treatment or restructuring strategies utilized by the structurally oriented therapist to bring about therapeutic change.

A second distinction is seen in the role of the therapist in the treatment process. Bowen advocates what he frequently terms a "consultant" role for the therapist; this is a position which scrupulously avoids "triangulation" and places the therapist essentially outside the system. The structural orientation, on the other hand, promotes the therapist actively "joining the system" to accomplish the restructuring task by creating a therapeutic system of which he is an important member.

Finally, a distinction between the Bowen and structural systems can be seen in their time orientation. For example, Bowen's method incorporates a strong emphasis on the investigation of the past and the understanding of "multigenerational transmission processes" by which family characteristics are passed from generation to generation. Structural family therapy, by contrast, places major emphasis on the present:

> Structural family therapy is a therapy of action. The tool of this therapy is to modify the present, not to explore and interpret the past. Since the past was instrumental in the creation of the family's present organization and functioning, it is manifest in the present and will be available to change by interventions that change the present (Minuchin, 1974, p. 14).

The structural approach has superficial similarities to the behavioral methods also. These are chiefly in the areas of therapeutic techniques, such as task assignments, and the emphasis on the present. Further comparisons are difficult, however, because, as has been pointed out previously, the behavioral approach has only rudimentary systemic elements.

Finally, most of the items mentioned in comparing the Bowen approach to the psychodynamic orientation (Editor's Comments, Chapter 2) are applicable in the case of structural family therapy; again, however, because the more traditional psychodynamic approach cannot be considered a true "systems" orientation, comparisons are extremely difficult. Indeed, the two approaches may be viewed as opposite ends of a continuum represented by a major emphasis on the individual, as opposed to an emphasis on the entire family system.

Raymond F. Luber

Introduction

Consider the following situations: • A teenager attempts suicide by swallowing a handful of pills prescribed for her mother for cardiac symptoms and depression. She is rushed to the local emergency room where her stomach is pumped. Her parents are notified by telephone. Within hours of the phone call, the mother makes a suicide attempt via a medication overdose. Who is the patient? What would be the most effective mode of intervention?

• A court battle is raging between two social agencies over the future of two young brothers, both of whom are diagnosed as emotionally disturbed. One agency champions the cause of foster parents, Mr. and Mrs. A, who had custody of the children for several years and now seek to regain it. The other agency reminds the court that the children were removed from the As and temporarily placed with a second set of foster parents, Mr. and Mrs. B, because the As were adjudged to be negligent and unable to meet the need of such special children. Their recommendation is that the boys be placed in long-term custodial institutions. How can one unravel the tangled threads of this situation? How can the level of the As' investment and ability to manage these children best be evaluated? How can the best interests of the children be served?

• A young, single mother brings her 18-month-old son to the emergency room on several occasions, each time with an injury that points to the possibility of child abuse. She denies hurting him, but says she feels overwhelmed and isolated, and that he often gets on her nerves. How can the child's safety be assured while his mother's ability to parent effectively is evaluated? How can support, assistance, and encouragement best be offered to this young woman?

The answers to these questions depend on the framework within which the situations are viewed. In a psychodynamically oriented treatment setting, where insight is considered a precursor to change, the mother/daughter suicide attempts would be seen as expressions of intrapsychic psychopathology in each of the individuals. If hospitalization were deemed necessary, they would be admitted to separate units, treated by different therapists, and each would work independently of the other toward understanding the causes of her symptoms. Although the therapists would surely recognize the concordance in the timing and the method of the suicide attempts, the individual, intrapsychic treatment philosophy would make it impossible to conceptualize the symptoms as evidence of family system dysfunction and to design treatment based on that conceptualization.

Similarly, the possibilities for evaluation and intervention in custody and child abuse cases are limited and generally result in either separation of the current family for the protection or evaluation of one member or subsystem (such as the young brothers in an inpatient setting, the toddler in a shelter) or dependence on sporadic home visiting to monitor the progress of the child. Neither option provides the safety of a structured setting, with the opportunity to observe the family in action, and to assist it in the development of more functional interaction.

At the Philadelphia Child Guidance Clinic, where treatment is systems, rather than individually oriented, we have answered these questions by hospitalizing these three families in our inpatient apartments. In the five years in which the apartments have been in operation, more than 70 families have been admitted for short-term intensive family observation and treatment. To the best of our knowledge, the apartments and treatment families receive while there are without parallel anywhere. We have, therefore, been free to operate without the restraints of precedent, and have selected families for this service on the basis of clinical intuition rather than predetermined criteria. In retrospect, the families we have selected have generally been characterized by failure to make lasting gains in outpatient treatment, chronicity of the presenting problem or related problems, and isolation from their social networks.

Many families respond incredulously, negatively, or angrily to the suggestion that they enter a psychiatric hospital for a brief inpatient stay together. They may need time, sometimes weeks or months, to think over the offer and work on it with their outpatient therapists. A smaller number grasp at the promise of respite from total responsibility, the possibility of intensive treatment, and are ready to move in immediately.

Intake, Assessment and Contracting

The active participation of the outpatient therapist, at the time of referral and intake, during the family's stay in the apartment, and through the discharge process, is a major factor in the treatment plan. As students of systems, and of mental hospitals as particular kinds of systems, we are on guard to avoid the dangers and incontinuities usually associated with institutionalization. Therefore, residence is limited to a brief stay, (the average length of stay is 18 days) to prevent resocialization to the patient role which long-term inpatient care encourages. The discharge process begins at the initial interview which also includes assessment of the problem, specific goal setting for the experience, the establishment of the time frame for the process, and concrete discharge plans. We explain our participation as a short period of intensive treatment within the ongoing course of the family's outpatient therapy. The outpatient therapist never relinquishes the family to us, and is encouraged to continue to see the family, as co-therapists with our staff member, during the family's stay.

The smoothest and most effective liaison with the outpatient therapist occurs when he or she is a member of our own clinic's outpatient department. When this is the case, we have the tremendous advantage of collaborating with someone who shares a family-oriented treatment philosophy and training experience. When the referring therapist is from another agency, the groundwork for collaborative effort is laid at the assessment/intake meeting which is attended by the referring therapist, family, therapist who will be working with them during the inpatient stay, and representatives of our psychoeducational, nursing, and child care staff. At this meeting, a formal contract is drawn up and signed delineating the specific activities and interventions which are planned, and the specific responsibilities of each of the participants in carrying out the plan. In addition to working with us while the family is in the apartment, the referring therapist is clearly identified as the long-term provider of treatment, to whom the family will return on discharge. This provides continuous support for the therapist/family relationship, and ensures continuity of care through the transition from inpatient to outpatient treatment.

Most mental health professionals share the layman's initial shock at the suggestion of hospitalizing an entire family. For those who are systems oriented in their thinking, the surprise is short lived, for the development of inpatient apartments is a logical extension of outpatient work with families. It is especially appropriate for those who work with the structural family model (Minuchin, 1974) in which the therapist's energies are directed toward assessing the observable operations of the family and including change in the family system within the therapy session.

It is understood that no therapy session exactly duplicates the behavior that occurs at home, but the approximation between the two is close enough so that changed behavior which is initiated in the session can be repeated and practiced at home. The inpatient apartment occupies a place somewhere between the therapist's office and the home. It is the best environment we have designed so far for replicating the interactional patterns of the family with a high degree of accuracy. It is also the environment in which the therapist has at his or her disposal an unusually wide repertoire of therapeutic maneuvers.

The Structural Model

The special advantage of the inpatient apartment for structural family therapy beomes clear as the outline of the therapy itself is fleshed in. Structural family therapy is present oriented. There is little time spent gathering historical data, reviewing past therapeutic experiences, or listening to detailed reports and how family members behave at home, in school, etc. Sessions are focused on the process—the essence of the family interaction rather than the content being offered. The attention to the present is based on the assumption that although the etiology of the symptom may lie in the past, the persistence of the symptom depends on its being actively maintained by the family system in the present. The past is not available to the therapist as an arena for intervention; it cannot be clarified, organized, or sweetened in any way. The present, on the other hand, is quite malleable. Once the therapist has joined with the family to establish the therapeutic system and been granted power and authority by the family, he/she can interrupt the behavioral sequences which maintain the symptom and introduce sequences to promote more functional behavior (Minuchin, 1974).

The symptom alone, when reported historically or talked about in a session, provides no direction for intervention, for it is without the living context that gives it meaning. The therapist must grasp the emotional climate in which it occurs, the language with which the family communicates, and the spatial and hierarchical relationships between family members in order to see the symptom as an integral component in a pattern of complementary behaviors. Among the common reciprocal dyads are the long-suffering victim in a painful marriage and an oppressive partner. Each needs the other to play out his or her role. Constant monitoring by the ever watchful parent is demanded by the irresponsible teenage boy, who, in turn, is protected from the consequences of his behavior by the smothering which he so loudly protests. The over-involved parent and the detached parent are a perfectly matched pair—neither could maintain his or her position without the collaboration of the other. Families often present as a triad composed of an out-of-control preschooler, an ineffectual mother, and a heavy-handed father who, while stepping in to take control of the situation actively, reinforces the mother's incompetence and the child's power. The scenarios vary widely, but they are there to be seen. The apartment gives us an unparalleled opportunity to observe them as they occur in the normal activities of daily living in a homelike atmosphere.

Similarly, the apartments give us an opportunity to work very effectively with therapeutic tasks. Tasks are a way of designing an experience of success for a family, through which their behavioral repertoire will grow and their perception of themselves as a competent system will be developed. The chronicity of the presenting problem of the apartment families and their frustration with attempts to change their situation means that they have become experts at failure and discouragement. Our attempts to counter this are greatly strengthened by the opportunity to work with them throughout the day, and especially through those hours of the day which have been most difficult for them at home. Although the apartments are not home, they do present a somewhat homelike atmosphere in which the families can safely practice new behaviors.

The idea of tasks has become fairly commonplace among family therapists, but there is wide variation in how they are integrated into the treatment. Sometimes the tasks are vague, given as a directive to "spend some time together this week," "talk with your child alone during the week," "do a household chore," etc. leaving the family with only a general idea of what is to be done. The behavior asked for may be new to them, and though appropriate in terms of a treatment strategy, may be outside their present repertoire. Sometimes, the tasks appear to be afterthoughts on the part of the therapist, tacked on at the end of the session as a sort of homework assignment, but bearing little relevance to the session itself. If tasks are used this way, they may be counterproductive, providing families with an opportunity to experience failure again, rather than to grow with the new experience of success.

In structural family therapy, the use of the tasks is precise. They are deliberately constructed so that the new sequence of behaviors called for are clearly relevant to what is going on in the session and to the goals of treatment. Tasks are always given in concrete and specific language and initially put into action in the session itself. The therapist's presence makes possible monitoring and feedback about how the task is being done as well as support for new behaviors as they emerge. Since the therapist's participation is considered integral to the operation, we take care not to send a family home with a task without the opportunity to "try it on" first and succeed with it in our presence.

The apartments are located within the Philadelphia Child Guidance Clinic's facility in the heart of the city. They are supplied with fairly nondescript, modern furniture and appliances. Each has a living room/dining room with a fold-out sleep sofa, a few tables and chairs and a galley kitchen, a bedroom with two single beds and storage space for clothing, and a bathroom. The bedroom is large enough for extra beds or cribs to be added when necessary. One wall of the living room/dining room contains a one way viewing mirror, through which the activity in the room can be observed from the adjoining observation room.

Each period of observation is preceded by the staff asking the family for permission to observe; and, each observation is specifically related to the goals designed for the stay in the apartment. For example, in one family treated in an apartment, the mother felt overwhelmed by the difficulty of settling down her four-year-old autistic son, and readying him for the transition from wakefulness to sleep. In this case, the staff arranged observations at the child's bedtime, both to observe what the experience was like for the family, and to work with the mother in designing strategies to improve it.

The life of the families within the apartments is as varied as the families themselves. Some adults leave every morning to go to their jobs or to vocational training programs; others are with their children in the day treatment program for most of the day. Some children continue attending their own schools and return to the apartment in the evening. Some families buy food and prepare and eat their meals in the apartment; some eat with the rest of the community on the inpatient unit. Whatever the details in planning daily life activities, the principle is the same; the areas of competence of all family members are identified, and healthy functioning is encouraged and supported. The assumption is made that the family members have coping and problem-solving skills which are not being utilized in the stress of the current situation. The apartment simultaneously offers the temporary relief of a protective structure and the challenge to try out new ways of dealing with each other.

The apartment offers a viable alternative to the predictable incontinuities which follow the hospitalization of the individual child. In the traditional inpatient setting, the parents' frustration and helplessness are intensified by separation from the child at a time when the child is in obvious need of help. The staff takes over and enters into lively competition with the family. It is an unequal contest in which the scales are heavily tipped in favor of reinforcing the parents' sense of failure. Yet it is to these parents, whose resources and skills have been unacknowledged and underutilized, that the child is returned at discharge. In even more enlightened settings, where work with the family is at least nominally part of the treatment plan, it is often the case that the parents' role remains peripheral, restricted to visiting and participation in family therapy sessions. They lose the day-by-day intimacy, responsibility and authority that they had when the child was at home, as well as any remaining self confidence in their ability to deal with the child alone.

In the case of the inpatient apartments, staff of all varieties and at all levels work closely with the families throughout their stay, but they are not induced into acting for them. The parents retain their authority and responsibility and are supported in their attempts to maintain generational boundaries between themselves and their children. This concept is so central to the work in the apartments that the only formal contraindication to its use is the presence of such physical or emotional disability on the part of the adults that they are unable to supervise their children.

The admission of any family into an inpatient apartment is marked as a crisis or a turning point in their lives. This is the moment when they are so thoroughly frightened, discouraged, or over-whelmed that they are willing to endure a disruptive and intrusive in-tervention. We make no attempt to minimize the sense of crisis or to suggest that we will take care of it for them. Our offer is to work with them to develop their own abilities to handle the situation. When a child is actively suicidal and requires constant observation, the parents, other siblings, and relatives, as appropriate, are a major part of the supervisory rotation and are relieved for periods of time by the staff. When the family chaos is related to conflicting or inconsistent parental demands on the children, we work with the parents to rapidly develop unified, workable expectations, but do not superim-pose our values on what those expectations will be.

The vulnerability of the family in crisis makes them especially accessible to therapeutic intervention. Admission to the apartment has tremendous impact in underscoring the family approach to treatment. By preserving the child's natural ecological support system, we allow the people closest to him to continue to meet his needs and strengthen the system to meet stressful situations which may arise in the future.

The use of the inpatient apartment has been widely accepted by referring agencies, many of whom do not share our treatment philosophy. They see it as an opportunity to provide a completely different, "last ditch" approach for families in which all of their usual interventions have not been effective. We are interested in, and welcome these families, irrespective of the catchment area and even the state from which they come, provided the referring agency or therapist will work with us throughout their client's stay.

In the recent past, the local courts have become aware of the existence of the facility and there have been a number of occasions on which entire families have been remanded to us for evaluation and treatment planning. The court-referred families, like those referred by other agencies, have generally had long and unsuccessful experiences with a number of public agencies.

We believe that our ability to work successfully with these families, to interrupt their dysfunctional patterns and decrease their dependency on public services will demonstrate that this service is both a clinically sound and financially viable approach.

References

Combrinck-Graham, L. & Gursky, E. Hospitalization of single parent families of disturbed children, Philadelphia Child Guidance Clinic Abstract, 1975.

Minuchin, S., Montalvo, B., Guerney, B., Rosman, B., & Schumer, F. *Families of the Slums*. NY: Basic Books, 1967.

Minuchin, S. *Families & Family Therapy*. Cambridge: Harvard University Press, 1974.

Minuchin, S., Rosman, B., & Baker, L. *Psychomatic Families: Anorexia Nervosa in Context*. Cambridge: Harvard University Press, 1978.

Chapter 6

PSYCHODYNAMIC APPROACH TO FAMILY INTERVENTION

Michael A. Solomon

EDITOR'S COMMENTS

Family psychotherapy and psychoanalytic therapy are two different methods. . . . Psychoanalytic treatment focuses on the internal manifestations of disorder of the individual personality. Family treatment focuses on the behavior disorders of a system of interacting personalities, the family group (p. 7).

This is the opinion of N.W. Ackerman (1970), who went on to state, however, that the two methods can be viewed as complementary rather than competitive or mutually exclusive.

The following chapter discusses the "psychodynamic" approach to family intervention. It should be noted that the two terms—psychoanalytic and psychodynamic—are frequently used interchangeably and synonymously. There are however, indications that this identification is simplistic and erroneous. For example, Nadelson and Paolino (1978) contend that both perspectives are identical in their focus on "specific structural concepts of the mind"; they differ, however, in the belief that only psychoanalytic theories and treatments are based on Freudian principles of psychic functioning and human behavior. According to this analysis, "psychoanalytic theories and techniques are psychodynamic, but not all psychodynamic theories and techniques are psychoanalytic" (p. 13); theories and techniques based on the work of individuals such as Sullivan, Jung and Klein would, for example, be classified as "psychodynamic" but not "psychoanalytic." The following discussion will utilize this definition of the term psychodynamic as any theory which is basically *mentalistic,* including psychodynamic principles.

This definition, then, means that neither behavior modification nor systems theory can remotely be considered as psychodynamic since neither focuses on structures of the mind nor attempts to alter specific components of this theorized psychic mechanism. Nevertheless, some important comparisons and contrasts can be drawn between these therapeutic systems.

Psychodynamic and behavior modification approaches differ radically in their basic presuppositions and orientations. Indeed, the two schools of thought have had several points of disagreement historically. These disagreements are also reflected in the area of family therapy. Behavioral approaches emphasize the immediate and primary importance of engineering changes in *behavior* in both individual and family treatments; their contention, generally, is that cognitive and feeling changes will follow behavioral changes. Psychodynamic approaches, on the contrary, contend that, in most cases, permanent change can be achieved only when *emotional insight* precedes behavioral change. Thus, psychodynamic therapists view the modification of underlying psychic conflict as a primary aim while behavioral therapists view the modification of behavior, that is, symptoms, as primary. As might be expected, this difference leads to widely divergent clinical methods and procedures as reflected in the appropriate chapters in this volume.

A second and related area of contention has been over the idea of "symptom substitution." Basically, psychodynamic (and primarily psychoanalytic) theorists believe that "if symptoms are removed without dealing with the basic intrapsychic conflicts leading to these symptoms, then there remains the *likelihood* that new symptoms will form" (Nadelson and Paolino, 1978, p. 94, italics added). Behaviorists, on the other hand, generally agree that this is theoretically possible, but that empirical evidence is overwhelmingly against symptom substitution. Indeed, behaviorists interpret symptom substitution as evidence of incomplete *behavioral treatment* (such as the suppression of antisocial behavior *without* the provision of socially acceptable responses) rather than as evidence of the existence of an underlying causal entity (Rimm and Masters, 1974).

Several similarities between the psychodynamic and behavioral approaches can be noted. First, both theories can be viewed as essentially deterministic in orientation. The psychodynamic approaches (specifically psychoanalytic theory) are biologically and psychically determined in the sense that biological drives and psychic structures are utilized as a single explanation for human behavior (Beavers, 1977). Alternately, operantly oriented behaviorists might be viewed as subject to a "learning theory determinism" while behaviorists of the classical conditioning persuasion can be viewed as also subject to a type of biological determinism (for example, based on their view of the role of the autonomic nervous system in the development of behavior). In either case, determinism leaves little room for the development of systems issues (Beavers, 1977).

Finally, a similarity can be seen with the development of increased interest in the family as an object of treatment. Both approaches have taken basically individual treatment techniques and attempted to apply them to a somewhat wider field, the family unit. In both instances this has led to significant attempts to broaden and modify basic theory. So today, we find a wide range of opinions within each position.

Next, it should be noted that there are some striking historical and contemporary interactions between the psychodynamic and systems approaches to family therapy. As has been noted earlier (Editor's Comments, Chapter 2), Freud defined emotional illness in terms of disturbed relationships and was cognizant of the importance of family interactions as well as the effect of early life experiences on later success and failure (Beavers, 1977). These ideas are considered by some to be latent systems elements in Freud's thinking. At least one family theorist, however, has viewed Freud's attention to the family in a less complimentary light; Ackerman (1970) states that "Freud judged relatives and family mainly in terms of their nuisance value. In his view, they posed for psychoanalysis the threat of invasion and contamination" (p. 14).

This, of course, is due to the paramount importance placed on the patient-therapist relationship in psychodynamic theory and therapy. And, it is in this relationship that significant systems influences can be perceived. Such principles as transference, resistance, the therapeutic alliance, interpretation and reality testing are elements of a well-defined two person system. This system has commanded a great deal of attention in the psychodynamic literature as the crucial element in the curative process. Indeed, this relationship can be the determining factor in the format chosen for marital or family therapy (such as consecutive or concurrent). However, as several others have observed (Ackerman, 1970; Beavers, 1977; Bowen, 1978), the patient-therapist relationship is essentially a limited and closed system. It is one in which boundaries are essentially impermeable and encompass only the patient and therapist. Nevertheless, this systemic element is a significant emphasis in psychodynamic theory.

Finally, it should be noted that, following Ackerman's suggestion, recent efforts have been made to develop a complimentary role for psychodynamic and systems approaches, at least on a conceptual, if not methodological level. For example, Rhodes (1981) proposes that the two theories offer different but not contradictory methods of conceptualizing the etiology and treatment of psychiatric problems. One is a vertical study of intrapsychic processes and explains behavior in terms of internal struggles (psychodynamic); the others presents a horizontal or transactional view of behavior (systems). At the least, this may reflect the type of adaptation and translation of more traditional dynamic theory which Solomon advocates in the following chapter.

Raymond F. Luber

Dynamic Approach

The dynamic approach to family treatment has its roots in psychoanalytic and developmental theory as well as ego psychology. These traditional theoretical systems have outlined the developmental progression of the individual from birth to death, identifying the stresses and tasks to be accomplished along the way. Under scrutiny, it becomes clear that almost all of the work that the individual encounters in the process of development takes place within the context of the individual's relationship with his or her primary objects (parents or parental substitutes and siblings) (Solomon, 1973). It is important for the therapist interested in the dynamic approach to family treatment to translate traditional theory into a family framework.

The oral strage of development and its concomitant anxiety regarding annihilation is mastered through an appropriate symbiotic relationship between parents and child (Erikson, 1963). The characteristics of this relationship must include the parents' sensitivity to the needs of the infant in both the physical and emotional arenas. In order for this process to develop, the parents must possess the emotional energy to invest in the demanding symbiotic relationship. The investment can only be achieved if the marital relationship has been appropriately negotiated and the needs therein have been adequately met. If the child is born into a conflicted relationship, the risk for poor resolution by the family of this important developmental phase is extremely high (Paul, 1965). There are a variety of other factors affecting the family which could also distort this progression of development in the oral stage. These include the loss by one of the parents of their own parent, illness of a parent, illness of the baby, difficulties with a sibling, etc. The point to be made here is that the therapist must come to the diagnostic facet of the treatment with a formulation which permits the definition of the problem to be expanded beyond its existence in the family member identified as the patient (Solomon, 1977). This process does not require the therapist to relinquish the theoretical base of psychoanalytic theory, ego psychology, and developmental theory. It merely requires more adaptive use of the theory which allows the family unit to be identified as the patient.

Similarly, the anal stage of development, which has as its major concern the anxiety of separation, is resolved when the family system is able to provide the security and object constancy which allows for more distance between family members. Parents who have not resolved their own separations from their families of origin are likely to approach the separation concerns of their own children with limitations and deficiencies. The treatment of their child in individual psychotherapy is likely to deprive the therapist of the opportunity to understand the full scope of the child's difficulty. Traditionally, treatment of separation problems in children has been approached by providing the child with a separate relationship with a therapist in order to minimize the effect of problems identified in the parents. This approach has potential for threatening the parents and reinforcing them in their ambivalence, rather than alleviating it. The dynamic approach to families with these kinds of problems would require the speculation that the ambivalence toward separation in the parents and this same ambivalence in the child, should be the focus of the treatment. In this sense, the system in which the conflict exists is the unit for treatment as opposed to the family member in which this conflict is most obvious.

In the oedipal or phallic stage of development, the same type of translation is required. The task for this phase of life requires that the child move out of the charged relationship with the parent of the opposite sex in order to identify with the parent of the same sex. Out of this process of identification develops a new capacity for a relationship with the parent of the opposite sex with less conflict (Erickson, 1963). Once again, the unit for treatment, when this process is distorted, may be the system in which the conflict takes shape, rather than the unit consisting only of the individual most demonstrative of the conflict. For example:

Johnny O, 12, is referred for treatment because of difficulties in school. He is unable to participate in gym class because he refuses to undress and get into his uniform. Johnny has academic difficulty in the sense that he refuses to demonstrate any aggression in his approach to his work. For instance, he gets anxious when asked to multiply or divide numbers. When given tests, he becomes nauseous. He refuses to relate to boys in the class and is most comfortable playing non-academic games with girls.

Johnny's parents are described as follows. Mrs. O is a beautiful woman with an extremely seductive way of relating. She is aggressive, competent, and self-assured. Mr. O is passive, somewhat dependent, withdrawn, and aloof. He spends most of his time away from the family, leaving Johnny and Mrs. O together. Johnny and his mother go shopping together and out to lunch frequently. Often, Johnny and Mrs. O sleep in the same bed. Mr. O sleeps in Johnny's room many nights.

It is clear from this case example that normal resolution of the oedipal struggle has not taken place for this child. The vast distance in the marital relationship of Mr. and Mrs. O creates the opportunity for Johnny to experience the well-known oedipal victory. Johnny has begun to deal with the problem by a regression away from any signs of development which would increase his capacity as an adequately aggressive, sexual male. The onset of puberty in this child was probably the precipitating factor in the development of the current difficulties. The family had some concern when he was six years old, but he seemed to "grow out of it."

Traditionally, the treatment approach to such problems has been to provide the child with a therapeutic relationship with a person who might offer a more appropriate model for identification. From this relationship, it is hoped that the child would develop an increased capacity to separate from the disturbed relationship with his mother and, perhaps, relinquish expressing the conflict through academic and social regression. Such an approach, however, has the risk of being fragmented in scope, as the etiology of this internalized problem in the child rests with the earlier conflicted relationship between Mr. and Mrs. O (Solomon, 1973). The therapist who views this family as a unit for evaluation and, perhaps, treatment, rather than Johnny as the patient, is likely to minimize the risk of embarking on a therapeutic process in which the goals may be so threatening to this family system. This could result in their sabotaging the therapist's efforts to assist Johnny. If Johnny begins to identify with his therapist and become more aggressive, competent, and individuated from his mother, the homeostasis in Mr. and Mrs. O's relationship is likely to be disturbed (Solomon, 1974a). Their relationship needs to be integrated with Johnny's progress, but this cannot be accomplished unless they, too, have become patients and understand the relationship between their marital problems and Johnny's developmental problems.

Those of us who have treated such problems in a traditional outpatient, child guidance setting or in an inpatient setting, know all too well that it is difficult to manage treatment of the parents so that it supports and enhances the treatment efforts with the child. Family treatment in such instances provides the therapist with considerably more leverage.

Similar translations of traditional theory can be made in relation to latency and adolescence. Once again, the therapist must understand the significance of the system in which a conflict germinates in order to make the translation. As adolescents move away from their families of origin out into the peer group and begin to negotiate with peers for need-meeting relationships, they carry with them both their resolved and unresolved developmental issues. Individuals then seek out other individuals within the peer group who will complement their own developmental accomplishments, whether positive or negative.

For example, if Johnny chooses to marry, he is likely to find someone who is tolerant and responsive to his deficits. Such a person is likely to have similar deficits but deals with them in a way opposite from Johnny. More simply, Johnny's passive-dependent, non-aggressive adaptation is likely to force him to search for a woman who deals with her own identification problems much as Johnny's mother did. In that sense, Johnny will recreate, in the present, a version of his own family of origin. His children are then at risk, as he was in the past. It is then likely that somewhere down the road, one of Johnny's children will be identified as a patient by school or mental health professionals. It becomes clear that just as treatment of Johnny in individual psychotherapy would have been limited, so would treatment of his child. The problem rests in the interaction between Johnny, his wife, and their child. It is this kind of translation of traditional theory that serves as the underpinning of the dynamic approach to family treatment.

In summary, the dynamic approach to the treatment of the family is predicated on the following assumptions.

- Individual development takes place within the context of the individual's relationship with the primary objects in his or her life, i.e., the family of origin or its substitute.

- Psychopathololgy in an individual may be a reflection of the individual's internalization or introjection of the deficits which occurred to the individual's primary object relationship system.
- Psychotherapy directed at the internalization or introjection of these difficulties should focus on the system in which these conflicts are sustained. This would include the family of origin, if the individual presents them while still involved with that family, or whatever family that individual has created into which the conflict has been transferred. An individual who fails to resolve a conflict within the family of origin is likely to create in the new family a system which will continue to tolerate and sustain that conflict.
- The psychopathology of an individual within the family becomes secondary to the intermeshing of the psychopathology of all family members that arrests the family in its development and interferes with their ability to grow as individuals within the system.
- The object and goal, then, of this form of family treatment is not rooted in the resolution of the conflicts of individual family members but, instead, the repair of the conflict-resolving function of the system. In the case of Johnny, the goal would be to provide the required relationships that would support Johnny's development as well as the continued development of both of his parents (Solomon, 1973).

Dynamic Approach to Family Treatment in an Inpatient Setting

The implementation of the dynamic approach to the treatment of the family to relinquish the identified patient as the patient and develop an understanding of how the identified patient's symptoms are reflective of the defective problem-solving process of the family system. This is extremely complicated and complex, particularly in an inpatient setting.

An inpatient admission requires that the family relinquish, however temporary it may be, their responsibility for the care, feeding, and interacting with the family member who occupies the patient role. In many hospitals, the existing program is antithetical to the treatment of the family in the sense that often, on admission, the patient is assigned an individual therapist, then integrated into an occupational therapy and group therapy program. The families of these patients are often excluded from the program and relegated to the position of providing history and only permitted contact with the patient at visiting hours (Anderson, 1977). This approach seems to institutionalize the patient's role as patient, and allows the family to defend against their own involvement in the situation as well (Solomon, 1974b). This frequently precludes the family's development of an understanding of the problems within the system. We have all been a party to some of the horror stories about hospitalization in which the hospital staff identifies with the patient against the family, and the family responds by sabotaging the treatment, or perhaps pulling the patient out of the hospital. In some situations, the family is only involved at admission and discharge. Frequently, when the patient returns to the family, the original difficulties recur quite rapidly.

It is therefore important that in settings in which family treatment is to be a treatment of choice, a total re-evaluation of admission, treatment and discharge procedures be done in order to expand them to maximize the effect of the treatment upon the family.

The hospital admission is a crucial juncture in the entire process of treatment, particularly with regard to the family's continued involvement in the ongoing psychotherapy (Anderson, 1977). It is important to understand that the point at which a family moves in the direction of hospitalizing one of its members, is that point at which the homeostasis within the family has deteriorated to a significant degree. The relinquishment of the identified patient is often indicative of the family's hopelessness. There are many feelings among family members related to the admission that are important to understand and to use later in the treatment with them. Often, the admission procedure is focused on the breakdown in the patient rather than on the breakdown in the system in which the patient's deterioration has taken place. This bias has important implications for the family's continued involvement in the treatment, as families are often relegated to a secondary position to the hospital staff as a result of the admission process.

These problems can be minimized if the treatment team views the admission process as a negotiation between the family and the hospital for help with a family problem which is reflected in the psychosis of the family member identified as the patient. This is in opposition to the view of the admission as the request by the family that the hospital "fix up" the sick member. The latter has its roots in the old medical model and is limited in its scope.

Hospital settings which are interested in developing an approach to the family must evaluate the admission procedure to maximize contact with families from the very beginning. Many admissions take place at times during the day when staff are unavailable. In some cases this is unavoidable but in others this is not true. Whenever possible, an admission should be postponed until such time as a family interview can precede the admission so that the treatment team can evaluate the family and establish mutually acceptable treatment plans and goals. When an off-hours admission cannot be avoided, it is imperative that any family member accompanying the patient be seen in order to set up a family meeting at the soonest possible time, making it clear that the process of treatment requires the involvement of the entire family. In this way, the treatment teams lets the family know from the outset that they are sensitive to the crisis the family is experiencing by admitting the family member with the symptoms, but also that the hospital refuses to accept total responsibility in the situation.

Often, the goals that families have for the treatment of one of its members and the goals developed by the treatment team are in conflict. These problems can usually be traced back to the admission procedure and the lack of a negotiated problem definition and a treatment plan which satisfied both the family and hospital (Anderson, 1977; Solomon, 1977). The following case example reflects these problems.

> Mr. and Mrs. J appeared in the emergency room at 2:00 a.m. with their daughter, Jane, age 18. Jane looked disheveled, appeared to be hallucinating and was non-communicative. Mrs. J seemed to be hovering over Jane in the waiting room. The family was seen in order to get a history of Jane's illness. Jane had graduated from high school three months ago. Since then, she had become withdrawn. Although she had a few friends, she had little to do with them. Recently, she has refusd to leave the house. Jane was admitted to the hospital and the parents were told that they would be contacted by the social worker on the ward. At 8:00 a.m., there was a call to the ward by the chairman of the department. Jane had called her parents and shared with them the fact that there were crazy people in the hospital. The food was terrible and Jane told her mother that she refused to eat any of the food. Mrs. J asked the chairman to sign orders for Jane's release. The ward staff was angry about Mrs. J's call to the chairman and were resistant to releasing Jane. They believed Jane should not go back to the situation where her overcontrolling mother interfered with her normal growth and development.

This case is not uncommon. The overdetermined bias in hospitals toward the identified patient results in limited data and a plan which often fails to understand the complex and broad scope of the meaning of hospitalization to the family system, and the family's conflict in relinquishment of the patient. As disturbing and disruptive as the patient may be, he or she serves a balancing function for the family.

Jane was discharged against medical advice at the insistence of Mrs. J. One month later, she was hospitalized in another hospital and the following dynamics were revealed in a family interview which preceded the admission.

The interview focused on the crisis that precipitated the family's need to come to the emergency room. Mrs. J had ordered pizza at a nearby restaurant. She asked Jane to drive over and pick it up. Jane refused to leave the house. Mr. J became angry and threatened to kick her out. Mrs. J tried to mediate between Jane and her father but was rejected by both. Jane locked herself in her room threatening to kill herself. In this interview, Jane was presented as the patient. The pre-admission interview, however, focused not on what precipitated Jane's behavior, but instead, on what precipitated the breakdown (need for outside help) in this system. The family was able to identify a high degree of tension between the three of them as well as a total frustration with Jane. They were concerned that Jane might really hurt herself and were helpless to stop her. The therapist said that they were all feeling depleted and were not much help to one another. They agreed, and hospitalization was suggested as a way to give everyone some time out and a chance to explore what was happening among them. Almost immediately, Jane and her mother became anxious about the prospects of hospitalization, with Mr. J staying neutral. Mrs. J said that she and Jane had not been apart for more than three months. They embraced one another and began to cry. They were helped to understand that they could elect to take Jane home if hospitalization was too frightening for them. With further discussion, they decided that Jane would stay at the hospital for the night and that the family would meet the next day to decide whether continued hospitalization was required. Mr. and Mrs. J and Jane were all permitted to go to the ward where Jane was admitted. They were allowed some time together in order to say goodbye and were able to effect the admission with relative ease. By the time Mr. and Mrs. J left, they were calling the staff members by their first names.

It is clear that the second admission was predicated on an evaluation of the family and the impact of hospitalization (Solomon, 1974a, 1977). In the interview the family expressed first their frustration and hopelessness; the therapist, sensitive to this, was supportive and offered hospitalization. Their ambivalence shifted to the other side in opposition to hospitalization, at which point postponement of admission was offered as an alternative. This allowed the family to look at both sides of their feelings, which resulted in a decision to admit. Optimal in the dynamic approach to working with families is building the therapeutic alliance around the decision to hospitalize. This interaction, focusing on an important change in the system, is often a preview for the therapist and the family of the process which is to follow. The therapist can test out the family's responsiveness to identification of their ambivalence while the family is helped in making the first significant commitment to the treatment process by assuming their responsibility in deciding whether an admission is indicated (Solomon, 1977).

In the first hospital, the decision to admit Jane was relinquished by Mr. and Mrs. J and accepted by the admitting staff person. This provided an opportunity for the J's to split off the part of their ambivalence which was in favor of hospitalization, leaving them only with their fear and anxiety about it. They acted this out by pulling Jane out of the treatment. In the second admission, this splitting was avoided by sensitively allowing both sides of the ambivalence to be expressed. At the first hospital, there was no attempt to help the family accept the hospitalization. In fact, Mr. and Mrs. J were separated from Jane in the emergency room. In the second, they were assisted in making the transition. They saw the ward and met the staff, making less likely their overdetermined reaction to Jane's complaints about the hospital. In many ways, the second admission attended to the issue of an alliance with the family, as opposed to an alliance with Jane as the identified patient. When the admission is structured in this way, the family and the treatment team are more likely to be allies. The homeostasis of the family is less overwhelmed by the second approach (Solomon, 1977). The second admission dealt specifically with the threat that hospitalization posed to this family. Their decision to hospitalize Jane for a day, which was later extended to three weeks, allowed them to make a minor commitment that did not immobilize them, moving them into the therapeutic relationship at their own pace.

The structuring of the admission process is also the first step in generalizing the symptoms of the identified patient to conflicts which are present in all family members, thus minimizing the value of the pathology of the patient. The J's were helped to see that the three of them shared the ambivalence about hospitalization.

Finally, the admission process, which is focused on dealing with the family's problem in hospitalizing a member, becomes the vehicle through which the staff is able to develop a positive attitude toward the patient and the family, minimizing the opportunity for an over-identification with Jane, as occurred almost immediately in the first ill-fated hospitalization.

In summary, the approach to the family where inpatient treatment becomes the choice, must include a structuring of the admission process so that it maximizes the continued involvement of the family, allows them an opportunity to begin to deal with their resistance to the treatment process, and helps them begin to generalize the pathology expressed by the identified patient. The admission should also allow family and hospital staff to establish an alliance in dealing with the problems being experienced by the family.

An inpatient setting is often a plethora of resources for the identified patients. Opportunities for peer relationships, recreation, therapeutic activities, group psychotherapy, individual psychotherapy, etc., are in abundance. Often, however, these resources are used indiscriminately with minimal goals. Frequently, the goals of the various therapies offered to the identified patient are not shared by the patient's family. As with the admission process, the evaluation and treatment planning process needs to be structured in a way that allows the staff and family to select treatment and treatment goals which are relevant to the problems within the family system, as well as the reflections of those problems in the individual identified as the patient.

This requires that the hospital staff and family explore the development of the family in order to understand how family members complement one another in a pathological homeostasis. Out of this understanding comes the ability to selectively use the hospital program to assist in repair of the deficiencies within the system of the family. This is not to say that individual psychotherapy or any other of the many programs available in an inpatient setting are contraindicated. The point to be made here is that the goals for the treatment selected are best established by the staff with the family out of the evaluation process. Let us return to the J family.

During the first ten days of Jane's hospitalization, the following dynamics were revealed. Mr. and Mrs. J had been married for 23 years. Mr. J was an only child of overly indulgent parents. They babied him until he was 18 but then kicked him out of the house. He joined the army and did relatively well with the kind of parental structuring that was available in the service. As his stint neared its end, Mr. J began to develop a serious drinking problem which resulted in a dishonorable discharge. He muddled along for two or three years unable to hold a job because of his alcoholism, but managed to avoid becoming destitute. He met Mrs. J, who at the time was working as a clerk in a dime store, living at home caring for her five younger siblings. Mrs. J, as the oldest child in the family, was not allowed to complete her education, nor for that matter, complete her childhood. Her father was an alcoholic, and her mother was overwhelmed with the management of a full time job and the care of her family. Mrs. J was attracted to Mr. J because of his "little boy quality." Mr. J's attraction to his wife seemed focused around "her ability to handle things." They both reflected on the first five years of their marriage as stormy, mostly revolving around Mr. J's drinking. Often, Mrs. J would go to work for her husband and covered for him during this period. Their relationship deteriorated significantly after Jane was born. Mrs. J devoted almost all of her time and energy to taking care of Jane and only concerned herself with Mr. J when he became drunk. He started becoming drunk more often. From the time Jane was three until the present, Mrs. J had been putting drugs in Mr. J's food. This would make him drowsy, and he would fall asleep before he drank enough to get sick or become violent. The J's stopped having sex when Jane began to menstruate at 15. Mr. J, on several occasions, made advances toward Jane during this time, which she was able to detract. In the last month, however, these advances had increased and Jane's resistance to them was seemingly modified.

The additional information regarding familial relationships significantly expands the first perspective of Jane as an adolescent with significant conflicts focusing on individuation and separation. This is a family in which the whole issue of separation, dependence, and independence has been unresolved for three or more generations.

Mr. J, in his family of origin, was encouraged in his dependent strivings but seemed discouraged in the development of his independent ones. He was booted out of his family with little or no practice at meeting his own needs independently of his parents. He attempted to postpone his independence by wisely choosing to recreate his family of origin in the service. This ambivalence about becoming independent led him to alcohol misuse. In this sense, as he learned from his parents, he continued to defend against his independent, individuating strivings. He met Mrs. J, who, in her family of origin, learned just the opposite. She was trained to defend against behavior and feelings which reflected her dependent and passive longings. Speculatively, they were attracted to one another because of the complement which existed in their respective adaptations. Mr. J represented to Mrs. J the dependency she herself was unable to express. She experienced that dependency by unconsciously supporting its sustainment in her husband's alcoholism and her daughter's inability to move on. Mr. J, on the other hand, was attracted to the independence and caretaking in his wife that he was unable to express in his family. He now supports her in this adaptation by providing her with someone for whom to care. This couple has significant limitations which they bring to both the caretaking and individuating aspects of parenthood. Jane, as the child of parents with these kinds of limitations, is constantly exposed to conflicting messages related to her own independent and dependent strivings. If she identifies with the conflict as it exists in her mother, she moves in the direction of denial and sublimation of her dependency, and if she identifies with her father, she may be required to relinquish her independent and competent strivings. Her ambivalence and conflict, added to that of her parents, has an immobilizing effect on the entire family system, and it breaks down with Jane's psychotic reaction as the red flag.

In the first ten days of Jane's hospitalization, she and her family were seen for five family sessions, each lasting one and a half to two hours. This kind of intensive beginning enhances both the family's and hospital's working alliance. The assignment of Jane to other forms of therapy was postponed until these interviews were completed. This is an important aspect of the process, since the beginning of psychotherapy other than with the family implies a contradiction. If Jane begins individual psychotherapy, she is, once again, given the role of patient while the evaluation seeks to allow the family unit to become the patient. Jane was assigned to a community group, the focus of which was to allow patients to set their goals for the day. In this group, Jane was helped to focus on her participation in the family evaluation and her use of the visits with her parents. In this sense, although she was in a group other than the family, the focus was decidedly on her relationship with her family.

As the family therapists gathered data from the J's, they were able to share that with the treatment team. This enabled those dealing with Jane to understand her problems as they related to her role within the family. In this way, even treatment personnel who had no contact with the family had information which permitted them to be sensitive to family issues as they were reflected in Jane's behavior. For instance, when Jane began to relate to one of the older night shift nurses in a way which suggested she was using the nurse to replace her mother, the nurse was able to structure her relationship with Jane to minimize this process. In this sense, the diagnostic evaluation data becomes a valuable tool for all treatment personnel. It allows them to preserve the family focus in all aspects of the treatment. This orchestration of focus and goal setting, so that family and treatment team are consistently in consensus, is crucial to the adaptation of a family approach to an inpatient setting.

Once the evaluation of the J's was completed, the family and treatment team were faced with planning the continued treatment. Technically, this is best accomplished by a special meeting between treatment personnel and the family, so that all may participate. When the J's evaluation was completed, they were still somewhat resistant to seeing their part in the problem. They *could* say that they remembered having "growing up pains" when they were Jane's age. They had not come to realize that they were giving Jane conflictual messages, however. They did believe that family meetings were helpful. Moreover, they were beginning to try to understand one another.

Diagnostically, this seems to reflect a beginning of the resolution of the family's resistance and the development of some comfort among family members that was not in evidence at the point of hospitalization. Perhaps what occurred via the hospitalization was the resolution of the immediate crisis for the J's. They were now in a position to begin to explore their situation in a somewhat less conflicted way. The remainder of the hospitalization, which lasted only ten more days, was used by the family and the hospital to further define the problem and to make plans for the continuation of treatment. Although the family was unable to understand the complex nature of their interaction in this short period of time, they were able to identify the following general problems.

- They were all unhappy often and could not share common experiences.
- They did not seem to depend on each other for appropriate kinds of needs, but, instead, seemed only able to respond to one another when a crisis developed.
- All family members believed they were isolated and barricaded from the outside world with not enough friends or social life. Even though the time they spent together was painful, none of them seemed to be seeking out other relationships.

  Out of this definition of the problem, the following treatment plan evolved.
- Family treatment would continue in the community mental health clinic with the therapist who began with the J's in the hospital.

- Jane was able to participate in an adolescent day treatment program at the community mental health clinic in order to begin work on her isolation and peer group problems.
- Mr. and Mrs. J were referred to a group consisting of the parents of the children in the day treatment program.
- Although Mr. J's alcoholism was of concern to everyone, the family believed this did not require treatment. They believed they could work on that by themselves.

In summary, this case demonstrates some of the crucial aspects of adapting a dynamic family approach to the inpatient setting.

The admission procedure must maximize the opportunity for helping the family remain involved in the therapeutic process and minimize the continuation of Jane's role as the identified patient. The evaluation period must be focused on the diagnosis of the complex intermeshing of the internalized conflicts of family members so as to be able to stage the treatment in a way that does not overwhelm the homeostasis in the family and create a deterioration of, or lack of, development of a therapeutic alliance. This process also serves to sensitize the treatment staff to family issues and allows them to participate in the unified focus of all treatment efforts.

Currently, many hospitals are faced with time constraints dictated by insurance companies or family finances. This case points out that a short hospitalization can be very effective if the goals for the admission are limited to crisis resolution, problem definition, and continued treatment planning. To set any goals which are more extensive would not be wise.

The coordination and integration of community resources is also an important aspect of adapting this approach to treating families. This is particularly true for hospitals that admit patients from long distances with limited access to family members. In such situations, a resource in the family's community can be utilized to evaluate the family dynamics in order that the hospital treatment team can focus the treatment plan. At the time of discharge, these community resources can be activated to continue the treatment. Hospitals should also consider earmarking funds in their budgets to cover the expenses of families traveling to the hospital for evaluation interviews, or perhaps covering the expenses of team members traveling into the community to do evaluations and consult with community agencies.

In cases where active family involvement is not possible for distance reasons or because their resistance is not resolvable, it is sometimes crucial to do a family evaluation to provide the treatment team with this expanded sensitivity to understanding the patient. This allows for realistic post-hospital predictions as well as realistic hospital goals. The goals for an inpatient stay must be modified if the system in which the problem developed is not involved in the therapeutic process. If Jane's family had not been able to participate in the process as they did, the staff might have considered a boarding home placement for her as a way to facilitate her individuation and separation. This would theoretically have minimized the regressive pull of the family and maximized her attempts to resolve her own ambivalence.

In this sense, a decision to *not* involve a family in the therapeutic process can be the outcome of a family evaluation. If the family is too resistant or if bringing the family proves destructive and non-productive, then a decision to develop a treatment plan which would make less use of family involvement would be appropriate. It is important to emphasize that the application of family techniques in evaluating and treating inpatients is for the purpose of enhancing the selection of the most effective treatment regime. It is impossible to decide against family involvement without seeing the family. Similarly, a decision to involve the family can only be based upon an evaluation of their capacity to make use of family interviews.

In summary, the inpatient setting has traditionally been geared toward seeing and treating that family member identified as the patient. This approach is fragmented and narrow in scope and fails to attend to the complex interrelationship between the psychopathology of the individual and the psychopathology within the family systems.

Since the hospital admission invariably signals the serious deterioration of the family system, it would appear that it is a natural setting in which to attend to family issues if the admission and treatment process can be modified to maximally preserve the family's continued involvement and minimize the takeover by hospital staff of family functions. Crucial to this process is the activation of community resources in order to insure continuity of care.

References

Ackerman, N.W. Family psychotherapy and psychoanalysis: The implications of difference. In N.W. Ackerman (Eds.), *Family Process*. NY: Basic Books, 1970.

Anderson, C. Family intervention with severely disturbed inpatients. *Archives of General Psychiatry*, 1977, *34*, 697-702.

Beavers, W.R. *Psychotherapy and growth: A family systems perspective*. NY: Bruner/Mazel, 1977.

Bowen, M. *Family therapy in clinical practice.* N.Y.: Jason Aronson, 1978.
Erickson, E. *Childhood and society* (2nd Edition), New York: W.W. Norton & Co., 1963.
Nadelson, C.C. & Paolino, T.J. Marital therapy from a psychoanalytic perspective. In T.J Paolino and B.S. McCrady (Eds.), *Marriage and marital therapy.* NY: Brunner/Mazel, 1978.
Paul, N. Operational mourning and its role in conjoint family therapy. *Community Mental Health Journal,* 1965, *1,* 339-345.
Rhodes, S.L. Psychoanalytic theory and family systems theory: A complimentary view. *International Journal of Group Psychotherapy,* 1981, *31,* 25-42.
Rimm, D.C. & Masters, J.C. *Behavior therapy: Techniques and empirical findings.* NY: Academic Press, 1974.
Solomon, M. A developmental, conceptual premise for family therapy. *Family Process,* 1973, *12,* 179-188.
Solomon, M. Typologies of homeostasis and their implications in diagnosis and treatment of the family. *Family Therapy,* 1974a, *1,* 9-18.
Solomon, M. Resistance in family therapy: Some conceptual and technical considerations. *The Family Coordinator,* 1974b, 159-163.
Solomon, M. The staging of family treatment: An approach to developing the therapeutic alliance. *Journal of Marriage and Family Counselors,* 1977, 59-66.

Chapter 7

Common Problems in Application

Carol M. Anderson
Susan Shilling Erstling

Despite the rapid growth of theories and methods of family intervention, few psychiatric settings have created programs which routinely involve families in the patient's treatment and even fewer involve families in formal family therapy. The problem stems from the fact that the basic assumptions on which family systems theorists operate tend to be very different than those held by psychiatrists or those trained within a medical model. Family therapists implicitly and sometimes explicitly assign a unique causative role to the family in the pathogenesis of illness. Most family therapists tend to de-emphasize the impact of individual psychological or biologic processes, believing that an individual with problems is a symptom of family dysfunction. Individual behaviors are explained by examining the structural and interactional patterns of the family system in which they occur.

Few psychiatrists or other health professionals operating with a medical model share this view. Psychiatrists view illness as intrapsychic or biologic dysfunctions which occur within the individual. The family, if viewed as important at all, is not recognized as an ongoing and influential context in which the patient exists, but rather, as a source of historical information or as objects previously internalized by the patient. Although many modern psychiatrists acknowledge that the family plays a role in such issues as the timing of requests for service, treatment compliance, and relapse rates, most underemphasize their impact on the patient's treatment and very few would support the notion of an actual causal role.

The divergent basic assumptions about the etiology of mental illness or dysfunctional behavior form the basis for a polarization of approaches that is not helpful to patients and their families. Family therapists are often skeptical of the value of such medical model interventions as hospitalization or psychotropic medications, and have increasingly chosen to operate outside of psychiatric systems. In fact, they have tended to avoid using such services even when there are indications that they might be useful or necessary (Haley, 1979). Psychiatrists, on the other hand, have often ignored significant research data and clinical observations which would support the importance of the family in the assessment, course and outcome of the patient's illness. The basic issue should not be a choice between a family and an individual model; rather, an effective integration of both types of intervention should be sought in the best interests of the patient and family.

Although the contributors to this book have demonstrated a number of ways to involve the family in treatment, an appreciation for the complex theoretical, political and economic issues involved is required for the effective application of these techniques in a psychiatric setting. It is the intent of this chapter to explore the problems encountered in attempts at application of a family approach and to provide methods and techniques for dealing with these problems. More specifically, this chapter outlines general principles for the application of family intervention strategies to the treatment of psychiatric patients. It outlines approaches and techniques useful in adapting family intervention to specific program goals.

Principles for Application of Family Therapy in a Psychiatric Setting

The success of a family program will largely depend on its appropriateness to the overall treatment focus of the larger program and its applicability to the patient population it is designed to serve. Nevertheless, there are certain basic issues and general principles which relate to all programs involving the family in treatment and transcend individual program mandates. A recognition of the need to attend to these general issues as well as to the design of specific family interventions will assist in ameliorating common problems. These major issues include: 1. an accurate assessment of the design and goals of the specific setting, including patient population, staffing patterns, and length of stay; 2. the need for practical administrative support for the integration of family work; 3. the need for integration of family data and family work in the ongoing routines of the unit; 4. the need for interdisciplinary cooperation; and 5. the need for training and ongoing supervision or consultation in family theory and clinical interventions.

Assessment of the Setting. In order to institute change in a system, it is first necessary to understand the system as it exists. An assessment of the goals, needs and expectations of a unit, along with an assessment of the strengths and weaknesses of current staff and their interrelationships, will aid in the selection of reasonable steps toward beginning a family program. For instance, the choice of family interventions will be determined by the number of staff available and the level of their family intervention skills. If few staff are available, it may be necessary to organize self-help multiple family groups to carry some of the treatment burden. If staff are unskilled, it may help to organize co-therapy teams or opportunities for self-help through videotaping.

Maximum integration of family principles into the existing program will be based on their usefulness to the goals of the unit. In most settings, this will indicate the need for a patient-oriented family approach in which changes in the family are instituted primarily to aid in the treatment compliance and improvement of the individual patient. For example, if patient cooperation with a medication program is required, family interventions, which elicit support of the patient's medication compliance, can be established. Such a strategy demonstrates the usefulness of a family approach in supporting the already existing goals of the treatment unit. The amount of time available for treatment also determines which family programs can be implemented. If rapid return of the patient to the community is a value for a particular setting, a family program is indicated which focuses on a rapid assessment of family needs and a reduction of family anxiety to enable the family to be more supportive of the patient and more cooperative with plans for aftercare.

In summary, whatever family interactions are planned must be clearly related to the goals and characteristics of the unit.

Need for Administrative Support. One of the most frequent causes of problems in instituting a family program in a psychiatric setting is lack of administrative support. Administrative support can be specifically translated into such concrete actions as allocation of staff time, scheduling of meetings, the integration of family data into the overall treatment plan, and opportunities for education and supervision for those beginning family work.

Family assessments or family interventions cannot be useful unless there is a consistent policy about the importance of the family which is backed by commitments of time and money. Family work takes more time than individual sessions, and therefore requires that case loads be decreased appropriately.

Furthermore, most psychiatric programs have work and meeting schedules which are incompatible with the needs of families. Meetings which are held during daytime hours can create genuine hardships for members who are attempting to work or attend school as well as demonstrate their caring for another family member who is hospitalized. Most families require evening appointments and readily accessible staff for support during crises. Adequate administrative support would involve the flexibility to create and facilitate staff and meeting schedules which encourage the participation of families. Without support from the leadership of a system, the effectiveness of family treatment is diminished, and work with families becomes fragmented and split from the primary treatment goals. Those in leadership positions must establish administrative policies which provide time and methods for integrating family data into the overall treatment plan, as well as administrative policies which demonstrate a commitment to inservice education and ongoing supervison.

Integration of Family Data into Assessment, Treatment and Discharge Plans. Family evaluations should be an integral component of the entire diagnostic process. Such evaluation should include an assessment of the stresses the family is experiencing and the resources at their disposal, as well as an assessment of family dynamics and family interaction. If the evaluation is conducted in a supportive manner, the ongoing cooperation of the family is insured. By bridging the gap between home and hospital at admission, one is more likely to bridge that gap at discharge. This process helps to avoid repeated hospitalizations, ensures continuance in outpatient treatment and the maintenance of patient gains. In some cases, treatment goals for the family as well as the individual patient must be established in order that the patient may return home to an improved environment. For instance, clinicians sensitive to family dynamics have observed that, on occasion, a family member will admit him/herself to the hospital in the conscious or unconscious hope of drawing attention to severe dysfunction in other family members or family interaction patterns. With a more complete assessment of the patient in the context of his family, treatment goals can be established which not only facilitate the treatment of the patient, but also the needs of *all* family members. Without such information, an accurate assessment of the patient is virtually impossible, and significant areas of treatment intervention are ignored.

Interdisciplinary Cooperation. Most traditional psychiatric settings today are organized to deliver services through a multi-disciplinary team whcih generally functions to attend to the different aspects of a patient's care in a specialized and integrated way. Through a hierarchical organization, clear roles and expectations are made explicit for each discipline. A family approach challenges traditional hierarchies and blurs the boundaries of such roles, suggesting an organization by responsibility, not discipline. With blurred responsibility, the need for effective communication and negotiation between staff is increased. Without good communication, those peculiar alignments and splits which characterize the families of psychiatric patiens are often recreated in the same alignments and splits between staff members. Blurred boundaries also require increased flexibility and tolerance for ambiguity in role definition and responsibility.

To facilitate interdisciplinary cooperation under such circumstances, it is necessary to demonstrate repeatedly that each discipline has a contribution to make to the understanding and treatment of the patient and the family. Each profession must be made aware of its impact on the treatment on the family and of the family's influence on the patient, *without* over-estimating their contribution to the detriment of the contributions of other professionals.

Training and Ongoing Supervision. An effective family program requires staff who are comfortable with families, realize the family's importance to the treatment process, and can intervene actively with families who are upset. Most staff of psychiatric facilities are asked to accomplish these tasks with neither the theoretical background nor the clinical experience enabling them to deal with the practical or emotional ramifications of involvement with families. Furthermore, few staff have been given a standard of "family normality" against which to compare the behavior and communications of the families they encounter. Since the only family most untrained staff know intimately is their own, any behavior which differs from their personal experience can easily be idealized or labeled as "disturbed." In this way, lack of training can contribute to the inaccurate assessment of family interaction. It is particularly easy to over-estimate the level of family disturbance, since families are encountered during a time of severe stress. Such stress may produce disturbed behavior, but disturbed behavior that is typical only of the unusual situation. A sophisticated family assessment is essential.

If money, positions, and trained candidates are available, staff can be hired who are sensitive to family dynamics and skilled at family intervention, yet who are open and flexible about working cooperatively in psychiatric settings. For the most part, however, inservice training programs must be relied upon to build these skills in existing staff.

The overall goals of such training programs should be to decrease staff anxiety about family intervention, demonstrate the relevance of the family to patient functioning, increase sensitivity to the needs of family members, provide specific skills of family intervention and provide the staff with protection from emotional over-involvement.

The content of family training should include at least four basic components. Staff should be given:

1. Opportunities to observe families and to interact with them in a structured way to gain an understanding of their needs and processes. People are more comfortable in new situations if they have structure. For this reason, we suggest that as many staff as possible be given specific, family-related tasks which involve them directly with families. These tasks may range from observing patient/family interaction during visiting hours to leading task groups of families and patients returning from weekend passes.

Opportunities to observe live family interviews can also help to demonstrate how certain families unwittingly support acting out or psychotic behavior in patients, as well as how the family therapist appropriately sets limits on such behaviors without alienating the family.

Active involvement and functional roles give staff an appreciation for family distress and increase the likelihood they will come to the aid of agitated, anxious, or depressed family members.

2. Concrete techniques for dealing with families which allow staff to feel less overwhelmed with the chaos that families sometimes create and prove that family training is in fact practical and useful. It is important to avoid placing staff of any discipline in anxiety provoking situations with family members without giving them specific skills with which to handle these situations and support in doing so.

All staff must learn what to do when visits between patient and family become upsetting and how to be supportive when a family member's anxiety is expressed in provocative ways. They must also learn how to respond when family members ask about the patient's progress. A family's requests for information about medical treatments should be addressed in ways that decrease anxiety and increase the humanity of the contact. Staff who are to conduct formal family sessions must be given strategies of intervention and conflict resolutions which can be used to diminish stress and discord between family members.

3. An introduction to family theory to provide cognitive integration of experiences and observations. A theoretical introduction should include theories of family pathology and basic systems principles, including concepts of family structure, boundaries and communication processes. Although many family theories imply an etiologic viewpoint, it is particularly helpful if this introduction to theory can be presented in a way that does not polarize a family approach with other models of treatment and force staff to take sides.

4. Experiential involvement in low-key family exercises to gain awareness of family dynamics and control of the tendency to impose one's own values on others. Experiential exercises which do not require too much self-revelation can be a valuable and enjoyable method of increasing therapeutic effectiveness, and a non-threatening and supportive climate can be created.

When new staff begin to involve families in the treatment process, they should be supported through ongoing supervision by those knowledgeable about family systems. Unfortunately, the staff struggle to learn about families is often complicated by the fact that those in positions of ward leadership do not have family training and experience. Most profesionals in charge of psychiatric settings are mental health professionals who received their education before training in family systems theory and family therapy were regular components of training programs. In such situations, consultation with family experts external to the system may provide the necessary expertise and support. Although this violation of systems boundaries creates its own problems, on balance the benefits may be worth the liabilities. If such consultation is not available, peer group supervision can be a valuable resource for the beginning worker.

In summary, there are four basic issues which need attention in the application of a family approach. Each area presents potential problems but can be addressed if one is clear about a treatment program's focus and goals. Approaches to each of these potential problem areas will differ according to the particular needs of a unit.

The following section presents examples of three psychiatric programs, each of which has a special treatment emphasis, and suggests how programs of family intervention might be integrated into these diverse settings.

Crisis Intervention Units

Some psychiatric units are organized to deal with patients in acute crisis, with hospitalizations lasting anywhere from one to seven days. In such settings, there are several specific factors that are relevant in incorporating families into the program. First, it must be recognized that the primary goal of such a unit is the rapid return of the patient to the community. All attempts at assessment and treatment are geared toward this goal. A family approach on such a unit, therefore, must include an assessment of the family factors and events which may have contributed to the crises and, thus, those factors which must be modified before the patient can return home. Many crisis units deal with the family primarily at discharge and focus on aftercare planning and disposition. In fact, it is much more important to deal with the family on admission. On admission, the family is upset and more open to help. By the time of discharge, even if it is only a few days later, the family may have covered over its needs and difficulties and, thus, will be much more difficult to assess and less receptive to a treatment alliance.

A common problem with family therapists on crisis units is the tendency to attempt goals which are too ambitious. The general goals of family intervention are the deintensification of the home environment and the connection of the family with appropriate aftercare services. Although many of these patients and families may also have chronic difficulties, these long-standing problems need not be resolved in order for patients to return to the living environment from which they came.

In terms of family intervention, environmental manipulation and very directive family intervention is likely to be the approach of choice. While providing an empathic and supportive climate, the staff must directly label the problems which are priorities, provide immediate active direction in problem solving and offer structured tasks and behavioral prescriptions which will reduce stress in the home.

Since treatment is to be brief, staff should avoid the establishment of an intense relationship with the family, particularly one in which their superiority over other treatment resources is implied. The tendency to form an intensive or primary treatment alliance with the family is likely to encourage the use of the crisis unit on an ongoing basis or even encourage readmission rather than the transfer of allegiance to outpatient caregivers.

For these reasons, the training of staff on such units also has a number of special requirements. Staff must become comfortable working under severe time limitations and the ensuing demands for immediate, effective action both within and around the family sessions. The content of training must focus on the effective use of structured, concrete and simplistic goals and techniques rather than on the use of insight-oriented or in-depth explorations of family dynamics. Staff must learn to give up ideas of "cure" or total remission of symptoms or conflicts. They must be comfortable with the role of beginning treatment and providing family members with a few coping mechanisms for use in a difficult situation. This is an important point since it is not easy for staff to learn to live with unfinished business and unresolved issues in case after case. It is frustrating for many staff to see people in acute distress and to be unable to offer help to them on an ongoing basis. Furthermore, staff become invested in cases and have difficulty giving up control of case management on discharge. This is exacerbated by the fact that staff sometimes lose sight that the natural pace on crisis units is a brisk one while ongoing treatment naturally moves much more slowly. A kind of unwarranted arrogance about the professional superiority of a crisis team can develop, which may result in goals for families which are too ambitious as well as in the alienation of other professionals in the community. Unless staff are taught some political skills about negotiating systems boundaries and the limitations of the role they can expect to play, problems are inevitable. In summary, treatment staff must be made comfortable with rapid assessment, rapid intervention, and rapid case transfer.

Since these interventions must be accomplished so quickly, there are special demands on staff time, energy, and ability to work co-operatively with one another. This requires a special kind of administrative support for family interventions on such units. First, staff must be assigned low caseloads, since it may be necessary to have daily or lengthy family sessions. Staff must have time available to respond to the emergencies that occur as families experience the crisis. Considering the inevitable rotating shifts and days off of staff members, it is also usually advisable to assign more than one primary therapist to a case.

Policies of this sort require administrative sanction, the creation of flexible work schedules and the encouragement or facilitation of communication between disciplines. This, in turn, will provide the necessary structure and support which will enable staff to respond immediately to the family. These requirements often create problems for administrators in terms of cost/benefit analyses. Crisis intervention units in general, and family crisis intervention units in particular, require procedures that are time consuming. Once procedures are time consuming, they become budget issues. Although such programs are very expensive in the short run, they tend to produce good long term returns. For instance, it is fairly clear that family interventions contribute to treatment compliance, continuity of care, and avoidance of hospitalization (Angrist et al, 1961; Esterson, 1965; Evans et al., 1961; Peretti, 1974). It is important for administrators to weigh these factors in the cost benefit analysis.

Behaviorally Oriented Day Hospital

The day or partial hospital program generally functions as an alternative to full time hospitalization or as a transition for the inpatient moving to full community living with a focus on rehabilitation. Although there are many models for day hospital programs, this section will focus on the adaptation of a family orientation to a model which is behaviorally oriented. A behaviorally oriented program is not the only model of day treatment which lends itself to the effective integration of family intervention strategies. It can, however, serve to illustrate some important issues which may be generally applied to other orientations.

The primary focus of treatment in such units is generally on current maladaptive behavior, emphasizing resocialization and re-education. Although most of these day programs are concerned with specific behavioral deficits or surpluses, they have traditionally assessed these behaviors through individual evaluations and as a result, treatment goals and intervention strategies have reflected an individual perspective. A family component for such programs can easily be justified. For example, patients need assistance in attempting to move out of the family home for the first time or may need support as they return home or to the community after an inpatient stay. Negotiations to establish guidelines for patient-family contacts may be required to enable the patient to maintain treatment gains and clinicians may need the family's support for the patient's participation in the treatment program.

The major problem on such units is translating behavioral conceptualizations and treatment plans from an individual orientation to an interpersonal one. Current literature in both the fields of behavior modification and family therapy is beginning to reflect such an integration. Although social learning theory has demonstrated that the most powerful reinforcers for a person are found in the behavior of others, the hospital settings have often neglected to use the natural resource of family reinforcement in patient treatment. Since the family or the social network to which the patient must adjust is a system of interlocking, reciprocal behaviors, it makes sense to assist family members in learning how to change their responses to one another. This process is initiated in the assessment phase, as specific assets and deficits in patient-family relationships are determined and used as the basis for treatment planning. The assessment consists of a behavioral or functional analysis of problems, which are then outlined in a formal treatment contract, written and signed by staff members, patients and appropriate family members. With the aim of generalizing treatment gains, the family can be involved, not only to reinforce individual goals for the patient, but to modify family interaction which precipitates or exacerbates dysfunctional behavior in the patient. In introducing a family oriented behavior program, it is helpful for the staff to focus on at least two categories of behavior: Behaviors that are maladaptive and environmental and interpersonal contingencies that support the problematic behavior (Liberman, 1970).

Since the goals of such hospital programs are most often related to "social adjustment" rather than the resolution of internal conflict, family programs should center on problem solving and a balancing of relationships among family members. There are two levels of family involvement which can be integrated into these programs. *Patient focused* uses family members as adjunct therapists who monitor the generalization of treatment gains or carry out specific treatment techniques under the direction of the staff. *Family focused* incorporates family communication and interaction itself as the focus of behavioral intervention, if such interaction is thought to be critical for the healthy adjustment of patient.

The goals for patient and families in a day program will vary according to patients' needs, ranging from negotiating the amount and kinds of family-patient contact for those separating from the families to regulation and modification of interaction between family and patient for those living together. In either case, staff, patient and family anxiety is reduced by the development of carefully chosen, specific behavioral goals. Once a treatment plan has been established, it is important to continue implementation throughout the day hospital stay. To implement the treatment plan, both the use of individual family therapy and group family therapy are useful. Family groups may be organized around the tasks and themes of specific populations, (for example, "Learning How to Live Apart" for those experiencing excessive conflict; "Effective Communication" for those who have communicative dysfunctions). There also may be education groups for family members who must learn to live with chronic patients.

Since it is difficult and time consuming to assess families, there is a tendency to assume that this need not be done regularly. A family program, like any other, can fail if it is not regularly evaluated and updated as new information is discovered throughout the treatment process. A continued analysis of the problems must be done to ascertain whether the initial functional analysis was accurate and, if change is not occurring, to determine if a re-evaluation of the problems and their reinforcers must be made. This flexibility is particularly crucial in the assessment of family interaction which may be highly situation determined. If family assessments are accurate and comprehensive, the family work will be seen as a useful component in the total unit's functioning. An effective alliance with the patient's family is even more relevant for day hospital programs than other psychiatric units since the patient leaves the hospital every evening and weekend. A family treatment component can make or break a day program. If the family is not involved effectively, a situation may be created in which staff, patient and family are working toward different goals and at cross-purposes. Wheeler (Chapter 4) provides many useful strategies for applying behavior modification principles to the family, such as reinforcement or reward programs, contingency contracting, and assertiveness training. These specific interventions will not be reviewed here. It is important to realize, however, that none of these behavioral techniques will be successful if the family or social unit to which the patient returns is not viewed as a significant part of the patient's experience.

As in other settings, administrative sanction for a family treatment component is important. The value of engaging the family, however, can often be demonstrated more easily in partial hospital programs than in those units where patients are totally under the "control" and "parenting" of the staff. Effective family work is clearly at a disadvantage when the family refuses to return the patient to the program each day or undermines treatment goals of the staff. Furthermore, since one of the underlying principles of the behavioral approach is the emphasis on the role of learning in the acquisition and treatment of maladaptive behaviors, a competent analysis of the patient's family background and current environmental influences are obviously necessary in order to provide comprehensive treatment.

Adapting the record keeping system to such an orientation is critical in the integration of an effective family orientation. Detailed record keeping is the basis of the establishment and attainment of objective, realistic treatment goals, the continued monitoring of treatment procedures and the coordination of family treatment efforts with other approaches. Many family clinicians have difficulty with the amount of specificity necessary in the recording of behaviorally oriented work. Therefore, administrative support in the form of time for record keeping and behavioral training is essential. A rationale must be provided which underlines the importance of specificity and learning principles to a behavioral family program. Training, then, must focus on a thorough understanding of social learning theory which views behavioral deficits as reflections of an individual's and family's particular learning history and the corollary principle that it is possible to teach the patient and family more adaptive responses. This implies that the role of the therapist is an active, educational one, a stance that is difficult for many professionals who have been taught to be non-directive or to elicit insight from families rather than provide suggestions. It is particularly important, therefore, that such therapists become comfortable with the direct use of power and provision of information. Modeling, practicing and role playing sessions making use of feedback and instructions with staff members can facilitate a more comfortable application of these techniques to family work.

A more serious problem on day treatment units is the fact that some patients have no families available to be involved in treatment. In the absense of family members, the staff must adopt a more flexible definition of family. Others from the patient's social network can be included; family systems principles can be applied to significant friends, roommates, or neighbors to support a social network for the patient. As day programs are increasingly working with chronic patients, the use of "significant others" in the treatment process must be explored. If the patient is truly isolated from even network contacts, a social network can be created to sustain him/her outside the hospital.

Inpatient Units for Adolescents

Some psychiatric units are specifically designed to treat adolescents and young adults. Since there is a common tendency to avoid hospitalization for young people if at all possible, those who are hospitalized tend to be seriously disturbed and have parents whose coping abilities have been seriously depleted. Furthermore, whatever the cause of the illness in an adolescent, its course and treatment is complicated by the needs and tasks of adolescence itself. The process of emancipation/differentiation creates its own difficulties as well as turmoil between adolescents and the adults with whom they have contact. For these reasons, psychiatric units which treat adolescents tend toward longer term care. This greater amount of time presents both more opportunities and more problems for a family program than the briefer units we have discussed.

On a longer term unit, an assessment can be more thorough and can be completed in a more leisurely manner. There are opportunities to view the family-patient interaction over time and under varying circumstances. Assessments, therefore, can be more comprehensive and extend beyond the immediate crisis functioning of the patient and the family. It is possible to give greater attention to other issues, (such as marital problems or problems with unresolved losses) that may contribute to the manner in which the parents handle the patient's illness or the patient's attempts toward emancipation.

Although the need for clear goals remains important, there is more time to accomplish treatment goals on such units. For this reason, goals *can* be more ambitious. There is sufficient time to choose and implement any one of the treatment approaches outlined in preceding chapters. Furthermore, treatment goals need not always be directly related to the patient's symptomatology or the immediate crisis situation. There is time to attempt to modify family patterns and structures, and to build skills in family communication in order to create a home environment which offers greater opportunities to meet the needs of the patient and of all family members.

The problems of enacting a family model on such a unit center around the over-involvement or countertransference of the staff. Staff over-involvement becomes much more likely with adolescents when hospitalization is prolonged. Adolescents can reawaken the staff's own struggles with emancipation. Younger staff may side with the adolescent, blaming parents for insufficient understanding, excessive needs for control, unreasonable demands for performance, and intolerable intrusiveness into the adolescent's private life. Older staff tend to side with the parents, blaming the adolescent's lack of judgment, manners, responsibility, self-centeredness, and insensitive search for an unreasonable amount of freedom. The long term nature of the hospital increases the intensity of the staff feelings and the intensity of relationships between patient and family. Over-identification with the patient can encourage staff to attempt to replace parents, and encourage the belief that staff could do a better job of parenting. Over time, it becomes more difficult for the staff to distinguish what is pathology and what is part of a normal struggle between parent and adolescent. The staff's need to protect the adolescent and to resolve conflict may perpetuate problems and prolong hospitalizations as they become triangled into family relationships; these issues are then given more attention than necessary. As time goes on, such irrational side-taking is likely to increase, usually to the family's disadvantage. Administratively, this process can be aided by the selection of staff members to specifically represent the family needs and concerns. A type of family ombudsman who is present during case discussions can provide a balancing effect on staff who may be over-involved with a patient's perspective.

Education and ongoing supervision also provide important input for staff dealing with these struggles. Although attention must be paid to specific skills and strategies, a greater proportion of training must address itself to the issues of underlying dynamics of both the family and the therapist and attempt to provide the therapist with protection from over-involvement in family struggles. Taking sides and imposing one's own ideas, values, and assumptions on families who are already overburdened with their own problems must be averted. In teaching, a greater use of experiential techniques which encourage the staff to become aware of their own family dynamics can be particularly useful. Role playing, family sculpture, and family photographs are just a few techniques that can be exploited to this end (Anderson and Malloy, 1976; Papp et al., 1973). Finally, periodic administrative reviews can also be helpful to avoid unnecessary, lengthy hospitalizations. Although these units are longer term, they should not attempt to attain all goals or completely resolve all conflict during an inpatient stay. When staff are intimately involved with family issues, a never-ending series of problems can be discovered and addressed. Case reviews by an objective clinician to determine the appropriateness of continued inpatient treatment can provide important structure for the overall program.

Summary

Although the field of family therapy outcome research is still in the process of developing research methodology, clinical observations and the results of research to date suggest that family intervention at the time of hospitalization can be useful. Therapeutic intervention with a family during a severe crisis or hospitalization of one of its members has been demonstrated to be effective in avoiding the necessity for hospitalization, decreasing the length of hospitalization, and increasing the likelihood of patient maintenance in the community (Langsley et al., 1968; Goldstein et al., 1978).

Although family therapists, such as the contributors to this book, have developed increasingly effective and sophisticated methods of providing such interventions, whatever family model is selected will encounter problems as its application/operationalization in a psychiatric setting is attempted. First attempts to begin such an integration are always the most difficult. It is generally best to start with small, carefully selected goals which have a likelihood of success and provide proof of the benefits possible through family work. The goals of some beginning family programs may simply be to complete a family assessment which enables the staff to adequately assess the context in which the patient lives, rather than to attempt to intervene and change it. In other programs, the goals of the family program may be to decrease the suffering of the family during crises, decrease their alienation from the hospital system and enlist support in the treatment of the patient. Other programs may attempt to prepare the family to accept a recommendation for family oriented aftercare. In those programs conducting actual family therapy, it is best to begin with a few particularly appropriate demonstration cases, rather than to attempt to see all families. A policy that requires all patients to be seen regularly with their families is usually unrealistic. An efficacious use of family intervention is one that makes a realistic appraisal of the setting in which it is to occur, the limitations of time and resources, and the appropriateness of treatment goals. While the assessment of basic patterns of family interaction and long standing family issues is useful in understanding the patient's relationships within a family, the short stays of many hospitalized patients mandate more limited goals for the patient and for the family as well.

Evaluation and the lasting acceptance of family intervention as an integral part of the treatment process always depend to some extent on the realism, specificity and attainability of the goals that are established.

References

Anderson, C. & Malloy, E. Family photographs in treatment and training. *Family Process,* 1976, *15*(2), 259-264.

Angrist, S., Lefton, M., Dinitz, S., et al. Aftercare: Tolerance of deviant behavior, post-hospital performance levels, and rehospitalization, *Proceeding of the Third World Congress of Psychiatry,* Montreal, Univ. of Toronto and McGill University Press, 1961, *1,* 237-241.

Esterson, J. Results of family orientated therapy with hospitalized schizophrenics. *British Medical Journal,* 1965, *2,* 1462-1465.

Evans, A., Bullard, P., & Solomon, M. The family as a potential resource in the rehabilitation of the chronic schizophrenic patient. *American Journal of Psychiatry,* 1961, *117,* 1075-1083.

Goldstein, M.J., Radnick, E.H., Evans, J.R., May, P.R., & Steinberg, M. Drug and family therapy in the aftercare treatment of acute schizophrenia. *Archives of General Psychiatry,* 1978, *35*(10 October), 1169-1177.

Haley, J. Ideas that handicap therapy with young people. *International Journal of Family Therapy,* 1979, *1*(1, Spring), 29-45.

Langsley, D.G., Pittman, F., Machotka, P., & Flomenhalf, K. Family crisis therapy —results and implications. *Family Process,* 1968, *7,* 145-158.

Liberman, R. Behavioral approaches to family and couple therapy. *American Journal of Psychiatry,* 1970, *40*(1), 106-118.

Papp, P., Silverstein, O., & Carter, E. Family sculpting in preventive work with "well families." *Family Process,* 1973, *12*(2), 197-212.

Peretti, P.D. Precipitating factors of readmission of psychiatric patients, *Community Mental Health Journal,* 1974, *10,* 89-92.

Appendices

The materials in this section are designed as illustrative aids and concrete examples of techniques described by various authors throughout this volume. The first section lists some of the common terms utilized in the family therapy literature; the editors would expect that this list might serve as a basis for the construction of a more detailed and comprehensive catalogue by the individual reader based on his/her own interests and needs. Other material in this section should provide the reader with a flavor for some of the techniques currently utilized in the field. As in all such cases, their applicability will depend on the specific characteristics of each situation.

Common Terms in Family Therapy Literature

This list is intended to serve as a guide for clinicians new to family therapy and its literature. Although concepts have been extracted from readings (with authors noted when the term seems particularly associated with their work) the editors maintain sole responsibility for the interpretations of definitions.

Alliances—Two or more members of a family who are united around a common interest or task. The issue around which they joined may be a positive task (parental alliance to rear children) or a negative one (mother-son alliance to fight father's authority). Also see intra-familial alignment.

Attributions—A ''hypnotic'' method of coercion and control of behavior (and ultimately identity) in which someone is encouraged to be what is wanted by telling her/him that she/he is this already. For example, parents may tell their son how he feels, or even tell a third party in front of him what he feels. Such attributions are thought to be more powerful than orders. (Laing)

Balanced Ledger—A concept of health in a multi-person relationship system or family (minimum two persons), as the balance of a long-range ethical ledger. The main dimensions include obligation, repayment, concern, merit, etc. Satisfactions for one member cannot be viewed without regard to the impact (justice) for others. Chronic imbalance is a pathological system. (Nagy)

Behavior Exchange—Approaches which typically structure therapy to facilitate the negotiated exchange of positive behaviors between individuals or family members.

Boundaries—In families, generally referring to the separating line between generations (parent-child) or between individuals. Well-defined but flexible boundaries are generally equated with health; rigid or diffuse boundaries are seen as pathological. Violations of these boundaries result in gross generational alliances or enmeshed (fused) relationship.

Coalitions—See Alliances.

Coercive Control—An inequitable exchange in a family whereby one member's behavior is controlled by positive reinforcement while the other's behavior is controlled by negative reinforcement.

Contingency Contracting—The development of a specific (usually written) schedule or contract describing the terms for the trading or exchange of behaviors and reinforcers between two or more individuals (Stuart).

Demystification—When an attribution (see above) has the function of an instruction and this function is denied, "mystification" occurs (values, identity enculcated by parents without child's awareness or choice.) Demystification involves identifying the misdefined issues through clarification of communication and use of meta-communication.

Detouring—A form of the rigid triad in which the spouse subsystem or marital coalition maintains the illusion of harmony by sending their stresses through the child. They may unite to attack him or unite to protect him, either way avoiding their own conflict. (Minuchin)

Deviation - Amplifying Processes—All processes of mutual causal relationships that amplify an insignificant event, build up deviation, departing from the initial state. (Maryama, Hoffman, Haley)

Disengagement—A transactional style of families or their sub-systems, which is characterized by very firm boundaries. The style is functional unless carried to the extreme in which very rigid boundaries prevent loyalty, support and interdependence when needed.

Door Knobbers—Those very crucial comments dropped by family members when their hand is on the doorknob, ready for flight. Particularly troublesome when one member hangs behind the others to share an anecdote with the therapist.

Double Bind—A repeated experience in which an individual, in an intense relationship with one or more other individuals, receives a communication that expresses two messages, one denying the other with no possibility of commenting upon the contradictions for fear of punishment, withdrawal of love, expression of anger, or abandonment so that it is disorienting.
Example: A child puts an arm around a parent who has hostile feelings toward him, and the parent stiffens. He withdraws his arm and the parent asks, "Don't you love me anymore"? The double bind for the child is if he is to keep his tie with his parent, he must not show him that he loves him but if he does not show the parent that he loves him, then he might lose the parent. (Bateson, et al.)

Dyad—A concept denoting two-person interactions or coalitions used in assessing family alliances, but which has more recently been replaced with "triadic" based concepts.

Emotional Divorce—Marriages that have the form and content of closeness but lack emotional bond, characterized by the inability of husband or wife to communicate their inner thoughts to each other. (Bowen)

Enmeshment—A transactional style of family systems, or sub-systems in which members tend to be undifferentiated, close, and diffuse. The boundaries between members are blurred. A heightened sense of belonging is gained by sacrificing or discouraging autonomy. The behavior of one member immediately affects others, and stress in an individual member reverberates strongly across all boundaries and subsystems.

Family Leader—A family member who assumes or is selected by the family to take on the role of peace-maker or protector in an attempt to rescue the victim from the scapegoating attack of the family or to turn the attack away from himself. (Ackerman)

Family Homeostatos—A concept denoting that the continuous interplay of dynamic forces within the family tends toward the maintenance of an equilibrium among family members, and which usually regards individual symptomatology as a manifestation of a family system. (Jackson)

Family Myths—A series of well-integrated beliefs shared by all family members concerning their relationships and which usually go unchallenged by everyone involved in spite of the reality distortions which they may imply. Myths may serve as homeostatic mechanisms; that is, their purpose is to maintain the "steady-state" of the family. "The family myth is to the relationship what the defense is to the individual." (Ferreira)
Common family myths: "Nothing bothers Daddy"; "Mother is the sick one"; "I only want what is best for you"; "Harry is just a child!".

Family Roles—A pattern of acts structured and learned in accordance with cultural values for the function a person has with his role partners in a social situation. Trouble can result from role conflicts that are not faced directly, negotiated, and modified but are avoided or distorted so that it seems as if one person is dysfunctional. Role theorists see "complementarity" as a goal. (Spiegel)

Family Rules—A concept developed as an alternative to "family roles" to study family relationships for the purpose of detecting certain redundancies—typical and repetitive patterns of interaction which characterize the family as more than a collection of individuals. (Jackson)

Family Sculpture—A non-verbal therapy technique where each family member arranges others in a tableau which symbolizes the way in which he or she experiences the family. The goals are to reveal family relationships in terms of space, attitudes, alliances, and under-lying feelings and to recognize defenses, particularly of projection of blame and intellectualization.

Functional Analysis—The process of determining what environ-mental and inter-personal contingencies are maintaining undesirable behavior or reducing the occurrence of desirable behavior.

Generational Boundaries—A natural boundary between parents and children dividing the family into two subsystems. The relationship of the parents, sometimes called the marital coalition or the spouse subsystem, is the unit within the family where the adults can meet their needs for sexual gratification and for compaionship. This relationship is separate and private from their relationship with the children, yet enables them to provide support, limits and privacy to the children.

Generalization—A term derived from learning theory used to evaluate the spread and durability of treatment effects; the transfer of learning to new settings.

Genogram—A pictorial chart of people in a family history marking marriages, births, deaths and illnesses, and used to examine relationships in the extended family complex. (Bowen)

Go-Between-Process—The positioning by the therapist in which he/she takes or trades the roles of mediator and sidetaker during conflicts in therapy. Intent is to apply leverage against "pathogenic relating" in families in order to break it up. (Zuk)

Good Faith Contracts—Contracts in which only non-problem behaviors are used as reinforcers; a reward (or penalty) is substituted for the behavior targeted for change.

"I" Position—A position in which a family member is able to "differentiate" himself or herself by taking action and responsibility for happiness and well being and avoids defining self in terms of others. (Bowen)

Intrafamilial Alignment—A concept describing the perception by two or more people that they are joined together in a common interest or bond and in that experience they have positive feelings toward one another. This is used to describe shifts and sequences in a family. (Wynne)

Intrafamilial Split—The perception by two or more people that they are in opposition to or have differences from each other with associated negative feelings. The alignments and splits within a social system define the emotional organization of the system. (Wynn)

Invisible Loyalties—The ethical base of expectations, the central motivating factor in families, the commitments to one's parents, spouse, children. Accountability with an action orientation. (Nagy)

Joining — (Accommodation)—The activity of the therapist which is geared toward becoming a part of the family system as its leader to make a therapeutic unit. The adaptive relating of the therapist to the family's style and rules, causing a relationship to be formed and the family to be receptive to his/her interventions. (Minuchin)

Marital Schism—A state of disequilibrium in a family in which both spouses are caught up in their own personality difficulties and hence fail to achieve complementarity of purpose or role reciprocity. There is little or no sharing of needs or satisfactions but emotional withdrawal from one another and communication consists of defiance and attempts at coercion. (Lidz, et al.)

Marital Skew—Family life is distorted by the rather serious dominance of the "psychopathology" of one marital partner. The distorted ideation of one partner is accepted or shared by the other in a kind of folie a deux or folie a famille—when the whole family shares the aberrant conceptualization. Usually in these families, one partner appears extremely dependent and the other strong and protective. (Lidz, et al.)

Marital Coalition (Subsystem)—The unit which is created to form a family and to meet the needs of the two adults for sexuality and companionship.

Mimesis—A technique (usually spontaneous) used by a family therapist to join or restructure a family by accommodating to their style, by adopting their pace, humor, affect, manners, etc. The humanity of the contact.

Modeling—Therapist demonstrates normal, appropriate, or desired behavior for family member(s), thus, offering new alternatives or support for effective behaviors.

Multiple Impact Psychotherapy—A method of brief, but concentrated psychotherapeutic intervention devoting the entire time and facilities of a psychiatric team to one family for a few days. It consists of team-family conferences, individual interviews, and group therapy and is particularly useful with families who might have difficulty committing themselves to treatment. (MacGregor)

Multiple Family Therapy—Three to five families with similar problems or who are isolated and can benefit from the support, sharing and learning of a group experience meet together for therapy. Originally, Multiple Family Therapy was used for hospitalized patients but it is now being used in outpatient settings. (Laqueur)

Network Therapy—The treatment of the social network or social "field" of a person by including friends, relatives, neighbors, and significant others in therapy with the goal of modifying the human environment of the patient. (Speck)

Operational Mourning—A technique consisting of the induction of a belated mourning reaction of a family member during therapy. Through repeated inquiry about recollected responses to loss, the therapist invites the exposure and expression of intense feelings in the member involved which may be interfering with the present relationship. The feelings stimulated in the others by such expressed grief are then solicited by the therapist in an empathic manner. (Paul)

Parent Effectiveness Training—A preventive child management training program for parents which has a particular emphasis on the effective handling of conflict and discipline by helping parents to encourage children to accept responsibility for finding their own solutions to their own problems, rather than engaging in power struggles. (Gordon)

Parentification—The subjective distortion of a relationship to behave as if one's partner or child(ren) were one's parent. (Nagy)

Prejudicial Scapegoating—The process by which a family reacts to a family member as being different from the rest of the family and whom they feel to be a distinct danger or threat to the security and values of the family. Sharing this sense of threat, several or most members of the family form an alliance to attack the source of the difference. (Aggressive vs. passive way of life; control vs. spontaneity; fat vs. skinny; smart vs. stupid; and habits of eating, dressing, etc.) (Ackerman)

Premack Principle—The idea that a behavior with a high probability of occurrence can be used to strengthen the occurrence of a low probability behavior.

Pseudo-Mutuality—A surface alignment between family members that blurs deeper splits or possible deeper affection too disturbing to admit openly. These members appear to agree in words, but, in actuality, are not listening to each other. (Wynne)

Pseudo-Hostility—The surface appearance of a split between family members, often expressed noisily and intensely, but which serves to blur anxiety about intimacy or deeper hostilities threatening separation. Both pseudo-mutuality and pseudo-hostility maintain vulnerable relationships. (Wynne)

Quid Pro Quo—(literally "something for something") An expression of the contractual or bargain nature of a marriage in which each spouse must receive something for what he or she gives and which defines the rights and duties of the spouses. The *quid pro quo* arrangement is not intrinsic to sex roles in marriage, but each family custom-tailors the marital bargain to its own particular situation. (Jackson)

Quid Pro Quo Contracts—"Something for something" contracts in which targeted behaviors function as reinforcers; specified change in one person's behavior is contingent on prior change by the other individual.

Reciprocity—The theory that relationships (especially marital relationships) function according to a cost-benefit form of behavioral economics in which participants exchange desired benefits or rewards on an equitable basis over an extended period of time.

Reinforcement—A stimulus or activity which results in increases in the strength, intensity, or frequency of the behavior which it follows (reinforcement may be positive or negative).

Scapegoating—The process of creating a deviant individual in the family in order to reduce tensions and disharmony in the family as a whole "one who bears the blame for others."

Schizophrenogenic—That process, be it mother-child, father-child or general family interaction, that can foster paralogic ideation, untenable emotional needs, contradictory models of identification or failure to provide models, leading to a schizophrenic reaction in a child. (Lidz, Fleck)

Shaping—Working gradually toward a goal by reinforcing successive steps to the goal (successive approximation).

Silencing Strategies—A kind of coalition by family members which forcefully and consistently is leveled against a dependent personality to enforce conformity and to possess an object on which to project their own bad feelings. Compelled to accept such silence, because it is better than dissolution of the relationship, the "victim" discovers the power in that position. "Victim" can resort to silence (or babbling) less and less selectively, resulting in increased psychopathology. (Zuk)

Spouse Subsystem—See marital coalition.

Subsystem—Divisions in families determined by the tasks, functions, or properties of the family or its members. Subsystems are most commonly defined by generation (parental subsystem, child subsystem), but may also refer to sex, interests, etc. Every member belongs to more than one subsystem simultaneously.

Structuralism—A concept used to describe family systems characterized by *wholeness* (denoting arrangement of the relationships, independent of the parts), their transformations (perpetual motion) and the homeostatic process (self-regulating system). Structuralist family therapy has as its goal a more adequate family organization achieved through manipulation and rearrangement of present patterns of interaction (sets). (Levi-Strauss, Minuchin)

Systems Theory—A model of describing the unity of a man which family therapists use, replacing focus on the individual patient, to explain events in terms of the relations among components or parts rather than just the sum of properties of isolated causal chains. Replaces the vocabulary of physics which had been concerned with one-way causality, and relations between an independent and dependent variable, through the use of spontaneity and feedback. (Von Bertalannfy)

Tracking—An accommodation (joining) technique in which the therapist follows and reinforces the content of family interaction, without challenging, for the purpose of exploring family structure or to intervene to restructure. (Minuchin)

Treatment Packages—The sequential ordering of techniques or elements guided by an overall model or systematic conceptualization of marital interaction.

Triad—A three-person relationship unit inevitably containing such processes as coalitions, alliances, cliques, mediations, etc. (Zuk)

Triangulate—An attempt by two family members to stabilize and reduce tension in their relationship by allying with a third person who can avoid intense emotional participation with either while still relating to both. In times of stress, attempts to triangulate take the form of looking for support or conflict in a third person as an attempt to avoid or deny such between the couple. A no-win situation in which each parent demands that a child side with him/her against the other parent, thus paralyzing the child. (Bowen)

Undifferentiated Family Ego Mass—A state in a family of conglomerate "emotional oneness," that is characterized by highly intense, fused, and undifferentiated relationships between families. Seen in families as husbands speaking for wives, mother's "feeling" for children, etc., and sometimes called *emotional stuck togetherness*. (Bowen)

Family Contracting

As Wheeler (chapter 4) points out, contracting as a family intervention technique is both a goal and a method. Contracting, to be a successful treatment tool depends on several elements: 1. identifying behavior to be changed, 2. specification of adequate reinforcement, 3. determination of equitable monitoring process, 4. clearly written terms, and 5. negotiation regarding terms and conditions of the contract. There are two basic types of contracts conceptualized and utilized by therapists: the "Good Faith" contract and the "Quid Pro Quo" contract. In the former, only non-problem behaviors are used as reinforcers and a reward (or a penalty) is substituted for the behavior targeted for change. In the "Quid Pro Quo" contract, on the other hand, problem behaviors are used as reinforcers for one another; in this situation, each individual involved in the contract must receive something for what he/she gives.

Examples of this type of contract and sample form for monitoring compliance with a contract are presented on the following pages.

SAMPLE "GOOD FAITH" CONTRACT

EFFECTIVE DATES: FROM JUNE 1 TO JUNE 7

We, the undersigned parties, agree to the following conditions:

1. IF   Joan completes all of her household chores by 5:30 p.m.

each day for 5 days.

THEN Joan will get private time to engage in one evening

activity per/week while Tom watches the children.

2. IF   Tom spends one half hour each day talking to Joan

about any subject or subjects she chooses

_____

_____

THEN Tom may choose a weekend activity for he and Joan

to attend.

_____

_____

Tom Smith

_____

husband

Joan Smith

_____

wife

Harry Jones (therapist)

_____

witness

QUID PRO QUO
SAMPLE CONTRACT

EFFECTIVE DATES: FROM JUNE 1 TO JUNE 7

We, the undersigned parties, agree to the following conditions:

1. IF   Joan completes all of her household chores by 5:30 p.m.

each day

_____

_____

THEN Tom will spend one half hour each day talking to her

about any subject or subjects she suggests

2. IF   Tom spends one half hour each day talking to Joan

about any subject or subjects she suggests

THEN Joan will complete all of her household chores before

5:30 p.m. each day

Tom Smith

husband

Joan Smith

wife

Harry Jones (therapist)

witness

CONTRACT MONITORING FORM

NAME _____

WEEK OF _____

DESCRIPTION OF BEHAVIOR(S) UNDER CONTRACT

NUMBER OF TIMES MY SPOUSE PERFORMED THE CONTRACTED BEHAVIOR EACH DAY

	Monday	Tuesday	Wednesday	Thursday	Friday	Saturday	Sunday
1.							
2.							
3.							

Multiple Family Therapy

Multiple Family Therapy is a treatment approach which incorporates the aspects and advantages of both family treatment and group therapy. That is, the family is present in the therapy sessions making both observation of interactions and direct intervention in behavioral patterns possible. In addition, the potential benefits of group treatment including mutual support, dilution of intense feelings and learning by observation and identification can be utilized. A variety of approaches to MFT have developed in recent years, most of which are designed to improve communication skills (Laqueur, LaBurt, and Morong, 1964) or problem solving abilities (Davies, Ellenson and Young, 1966).

One structured short-term, educationally based approach described by Luber and Wells (1977) attempted to provide participants with tools to develop new behavior patterns based on greater emotional individuation. The approach placed emphases on the application and rehearsal of didactic material by families and family members. A total of seven 90 minute sessions were constructed each utilizing a specific technique or theme. Table 1 briefly outlines the aims and techniques used in this particular approach.

Other MFT approaches have been described in the literature which are less structured, more open-ended and not based on the educational approach used by Luber and Wells. The program described above, however, may have some advantages in situations in which MFT is being incorporated for the first time or where staff are unfamiliar with the theory and techniques of MFT. In addition, this approach can be adapted to fit individual circumstances and can provide for the collection of data to objectively evaluate its efficacy.

References

Davies, T., Ellenson, G., & Young, R. Therapy with a group of families in a psychiatric day center. *American Journal of Orthopsychiatry*, 1966, *36*, 134-146.

Laqueur, H.P., LaBurt, H.A., & Morong, E. Multiple family therapy. In J.H. Masserman (Ed.), *Current Psychiatric Therapies*. NY: Grune & Stratton, 1964.

Luber, R.F., & Wells, R.A. Structured, short-term multiple family therapy: An educational approach. *International Journal of Group Psychotherapy*, 1977, *27*, 43-58.

Strelnick, A.H. Multiple family group therapy: A review of the literature. *Family Therapy*, 1977, *16*, 307-325.

Table 1: Multiple Family Therapy (Luber and Wells, 1977)

SESSION	THEMES	AIMS	TECHNIQUES
1.	INTRODUCTION	• Promote cohesion • Explain purpose • Present teaching material	• Round robin introductions • Definition of basic terms • Diagrams and handouts • Rating scales
2.	Patterns of Expectation and Obligation	Explore the explicit expectations family members have on one another.	• Poetry (Emily Dickinson) • Group and family subgroup discussions.
3.	Roles and role functions of family members.	Label family members' roles and receive feedback.	• "Square Completion Game" (mixed family groups). • "Lecture" on roles. • Mother, father, sibling subgroup discussions. • Family groups.
4. & 5.	Communication Techniques "empathic understanding" skills	Provide didactic material and rehearsal of empathic techniques.	• Lecture material • Structured exercises
6.	Multi-generational patterns in families	Demonstrate repeated family patterns.	• Family sculpting
7.	Termination	• Review and consolidate • Evaluate session	• Session-by-session review • Rating scales and verbal evaluation

Family Sculpting

"Family sculpting is a therapeutic art form in which each family member arranges other members in a tableau which physically symbolizes their emotional relationship with one another" (Papp, Silverstein, and Carter, 1973). In this technique a visual picture of the action and feelings within a family is produced utilizing posture and spacial relationships.

Proponents of sculpting indicate that it has several major advantages including: 1. the objectification of aspects of family life, thus, avoiding intellectualization, defensiveness and blame; 2. the adhesion of families in that it forces members to see themselves as part of a unit which affects every other part; and, 3. the physical representation of relationships and feelings which can provide a springboard for change by providing the basis for future relationship realignment (Papp et al, 1973; Papp, 1973).

Several examples of sculpting are described in the literature and will be briefly summarized here to indicate how this technique is utilized.

In one family group, the father was characterized as the "Rock of Gibraltar" which supported the entire family. To visualize this, one family member placed the father bending over backwards, supporting the family with one hand and three businesses with another; another family member placed him in a position in which he was lecturing sternly with a pointed finger; and a third member placed him on a pedestal with all other family members looking up to him for guidance. The father, himself, had a different perception: he placed himself flat on the floor stating he was swimming upstream in mud; he then placed his wife so that she was hanging on to his feet, a child hanging onto her feet and another child across his neck like a mill stone. These tableaus, as well as possible changes in relationships, served as discussion material in the therapy session.

In other groups (Luber and Wells, 1977) sculpting has been used to depict multigenerational patterns in families. For example, one mother was asked to sculpt her family of origin and visually depict their emotional relationships. She placed her father in one room reading, her mother in the kitchen, her brother in another room alone playing cards and depicted herself moving from room to room trying to engage someone in conversation. When asked to depict her nuclear family she placed her husband in the living room, herself in the kitchen, her daughter (who was, at that point, the identified patient) wandering from place to place trying to gain someone's attention. To further objectify these representations, Polaroid pictures were taken of each sculpting and compared and discussion as part of the treatment session.

How To Do Family Sculpting

1. Choose one family member to set up a sculpture making certain he/she understands it is how *he/she* experiences or feels it, not the ideal.
2. Ask each member how they feel in the position to which they have been assigned. (Sometimes people will indicate that the position in which they have been placed isn't right. Ask them to save the idea and you will give them an opportunity to sculpt; for now, they are to say how they feel as the other family member has placed them).
3. Check each participant in the sculpting to see if they are aware of how others perceived them—whether they are surprised, disappointed, angry, etc.
4. If you have extra people (observers, co-therapists, group members) ask for their feelings as well. Sometimes this will get family members moving out of stereotyped responses.
5. In the end, get people to talk about the whole experience and evaluate it. Try to have them make connections or help each other with insights. Generally speaking, it doesn't help to share your own insights unless they come from the family naturally.

Variations

1. Ask the person who is doing the sculpture to have each person make a "typical comment" after he places them in their position.
2. Ask the person who is doing the sculpture to play each person and tell how it feels.
3. Ask the person doing the sculpture to give the family a message as he finishes.
4. Try a composite picture (emphasizing contradictions).
5. Do a sculpture of three generations, examining relationship patterns transmitted over the years, and the impact of dramatic events such as births, deaths, and marriages.

References

Luber, R.F. & Wells, R.A. Structured, short-term multiple family therapy: An educational approach. *International Journal of Group Psychotherapy*, 1977, *27*, 43-58.

Papp, P. Sculpting the family. *The Family*, 1973, *1*, 44-48.
Papp, P., Silverstein, O., & Carter, E. Family sculpting in preventive work with "well families." *Family Process*, 1973, *12*, 197-212.

FAMILY INFORMATION QUESTIONNAIRE (I)

Date: _____

1. General

   Name: _____

   Address: _____

   Age: _____ Telephone No. _____

   Occupation: _____

   With whom are you now living? (list people)_____

   _____

   Do you live in a house, room, apartment, etc.? _____

   _____

2. Marital History

   How long did you know your marriage partner before engagement? _____

   For how long were you engaged? _____

   Husband's/Wife's age_____

   Husband's/Wife's occupation _____

   Husband's/Wife's personality (in your own words) _____

   _____

3. In what areas is there compatibility? _____

   _____

   _____

4. How do you get along with your in-laws? (This includes brothers- and sisters-in-law.) _____

   _____

   _____

5. How many children do you have? _____

_____

6. Give details of any previous marriage: _____

_____

_____

_____

7. Family Data
    (a) Father
    Name: _____ If deceased, cause of death: _____
    Age: _____ Your age at the time: _____
    Occupation: _____
    Health: _____
    (b) Mother
    Name: _____ If deceased, cause of death: _____
    Age: _____ Your age at the time: _____
    Occupation: _____
    Health: _____
    (c) Siblings
    Brothers, (names, ages, occupations. Indicate whether they are
    single, married, divorced, etc.): _____

    _____

    _____

    Sisters, (names, ages, occupations. Indicate whether they are
    single, married, divorced, etc.): _____

    _____

    _____

8. Relationship with brothers and sisters:
    (a) Past: _____

    _____

    _____

    _____

(b) Present: _____

_____

_____

_____

9. Give a description of your father's personality and his attitude toward you (past and present): _____

_____

10. Give a description of your mother's personality and her attitude toward you (past and present): _____

_____

11. In what ways were you punished by your parents as a child?

_____

_____

12. Give an impression of your home atmosphere (i.e., the home in which you grew up. Mention state of compatibility between parents and between parents and children). _____

_____

_____

13. Were you able to confide in your parents? _____

14. If you have a stepparent, give your age when parent remarried.

_____

15. Give an outline of your religious training. _____

_____

16. If you were not brought up by your parents, who did bring you up and between what years?_____

17. Has anyone (parents, relatives, friends) ever interfered in your marriage, occupation, etc. _____

_____

18. Who are the most important people in your life? _____

_____

_____

_____

19. Does any member of your family suffer from alcoholism, epilepsy, or anything which can be considered a "mental disorder"? _____

_____

_____

_____

20. Are there any other members of the family about whom information regarding illness, etc. is relevant? _____

_____

FAMILY INFORMATION QUESTIONNAIRE (II)

(This type of questionnaire can be useful in eliciting information regarding interactional patterns, roles, alliances, etc. when administered to individual family members.)

1. Describe in as much detail as you can what happens at a typical evening meal.
2. Choose a special holiday (such as Christmas, Thanksgiving, or a birthday) and describe how it is celebrated by the family.
3. Describe an argument you had at home recently including what started it, who was involved, what happened and how it turned out.
4. What does each family member like to do in his/her spare time?
5. In every family different members have different characteristics. In your family who is the bossiest, the biggest trouble maker, the one who gets away with murder, the biggest crybaby, the workhorse, etc?
6. What does each member of the family do that pleases you the most and makes you feel good? What do they do that makes you unhappy and angry?
7. What is the earliest thing in your life that you can remember?
8. If you could change one thing about each member of your family what would you change?
9. If you could change one thing about yourself what would you change?
10. What do you think is the major problem in your family relationship and how does it affect you?

PLANNED PASSES AND HOME VISITS

RATIONALE:

After any psychiatric hospitalization, but particularly after lengthy ones, there is a difficult period of adjustment for patients and their families. Usually, the patient has been hospitalized after a period of turmoil, leaving both patient and family uncomfortable about the patient's abilities and their relationship with one another. Although most families visit during the patient's hospitalization, and in many cases family therapy sessions occur, it is important to provide a chance for the family to be together under increasingly natural circumstances to provide a gradual reintegration of the patient. Planned visits between the patient and his family are one method of beginning to reintegrate the patient into his community. These sessions should move from highly structured contacts to contacts of increasing spontaneity.

GOALS:

Diagnostic: These visits can highlight problem areas in family relationships, in the patient's ability to tolerate various aspects of family life, and in the family's ability to tolerate patient behaviors. This in turn can provide a focus for inhospital and aftercare treatment.

Therapeutic: These visits can involve specific tasks which will desensitize patients and their families to fears and discomforts about the patient returning home and begin to establish reasonable expectations and structure for home interaction on an ongoing basis.

HOW TO SET IT UP:

The most important thing in establishing a reasonable series of home visits is that they be carefully planned and evaluated. This means beginning with very short, structured visits, gradually increasing in duration and decreasing in structure.

For this reason, such a program should begin with a meeting during which therapist, patient, and family discuss a mutually acceptable plan for a visit not to exceed two to three hours in duration. It should involve a very specific activity such as lunch or dinner within walking distance of the hospital. If family relationships are potentially volatile, topics for conversation can be outlined in advance, with troublesome issues declared "off limits." Both patient and family are instructed that the visit may be terminated at any point when trouble occurs or when anyone begins to feel uncomfortable.

EVALUATION:

It is most important that the visit be discussed or "rehashed" *whether or not* it "goes well." The specifics of what went wrong or the specifics of what made it successful are both important data for treatment planning.

It is very important that each person's view of the visit be elicited, and that candor be encouraged. Some questions that aid in discussions include:

1. What general things did you do? Talk about?
2. Were there things about the visit that went particularly well?
3. Were there things about the visit that made you uncomfortable?
4. Were there things you did not feel free to say during the visit?
5. If you had wanted to, would you have been able to ask to end the visit prematurely?
6. If you had it to do over, would you plan it differently?
7. Did you discover anything about yourself or your relationships that you were not aware of before the visit?
8. Considering this visit, how should we plan the next visit?

If the visit went well, the next visit can involve a longer time period, include less structured time spent in the home or include discussions of more controversial topics. If the visit did not go well, the next visit is planned to be shorter or more carefully structured.

INDEX

Author Index

Ackerman, N. 102, 104, 119, 141
Agras, W. 79, 90
Anderson, C. 12, 14, 16, 18, 23, 27, 110, 111, 119, 135, 137
Angrist, S. 130, 137
Appleton, W. 17, 27
Authier, J. 67

Bateson, G. 140
Beavers, W. 104, 119
Bowen, M. 30, 32, 33, 36, 38, 41, 104, 119, 140, 142, 147
Boud, J. 22, 27
Brady, J. 79, 90
Brown, B. 25, 28
Butz, G. 76, 89

Carkhuff, R. 49, 67
Carter, E. 154, 156
Chagoya, L. 20, 27
Coufal, J. 57, 67

Davies, D. 13, 27, 152
Davis, J. 86, 90
De Witt, K. 9, 10, 27
Dezen, A. 9, 10, 28
DeRisi, W. 76, 89
Dies, R. 10, 28
Durkheim, E. 44, 47

Eckman, T. 87, 89
Ellenson, G. 13, 27, 152
Entin, A. 44, 47
Erikson, E. 105, 106, 120

Esterson, J. 130, 137
Evans, A. 130, 137
Evans, H. 20, 27
Evans, J. 16, 27

Ferreira, H. 141
Fleck, S. 146
Framo, J. 35, 47

Ginsberg, B. 57, 67
Glick, D. 10, 27
Goldfarb, A. 82, 86, 89
Goldstein, A. 67
Goldstein, M. 16, 27, 136, 137
Goren, S. 12
Gould, E. 10, 27
Gralnick, A. 10, 23, 28
GAP 9, 27, 33, 47
Guerney, B. 10, 13, 27, 52, 56, 57, 68
Gurman, A. 10, 27, 50, 68, 70, 90
Guttman, H. 19, 27

Haley, J. 122, 137, 139
Hamerlynck, L. 10, 28, 69, 90
Handy, L. 10, 28, 69, 90
Harrel, J. 13, 28
Hoffman, L. 139

Jackson, D. 141

Kniskern, D. 10, 27, 50, 68, 70, 90

Subject Index

of family member, 18
partial, 16, 22
psychiatric, multiple, 20
 inpatient, 22
 outpatient, 22
 repeated, 124
 short-term, 16
Hospitalized patients
 with affective disorders, 44
 chronically psychotic, 86
 functioning of, 42

Identified patient, 5, 9, 10, 12,
 13, 16, 19, 46, 84, 111, 114, 118
 emotional stability of, 18
 mental status of, 18
Imagery, 80
Instigation therapy, 77-78
Institutional settings,
 advantages of, 86-88
Initial interview, 95
Intake, 95-97
Inpatient
 apartment, 97, 100
 hospitalization, 16
 service, 20, 23
 setting, 14
  demands of, 86
 staff, 25
 units, 22
  for adolescents, 133-135
 ward, 21
Interdisciplinary cooperation, 128
Intervention, 69, 92
 crisis, 128-130
 effective mode of, 94
 family, 121, 126
  directive, 128
 at hospitalization, 136
 short-term, 95, 97
 ntervention, 121
 ntrapsychic forces, 31
  in Bowen theory, 31,
  in structural approach, 31

_earning theory
 in behavior modification, 71, 88

and determinism, 104
orientation, 69
Marital therapy, 9, 49,
 71, 104
Medical model, 26, 110, 121, 122
 issues, 34-36
Mode switching, 54
Model for identification, 107
Modification of behavior, 70
Mother-child symbiosis, 29
 as system, 29
Multiple family formation, 61
Multiple family therapy, 152, 153

NIMH research program, 33

Oedipal conflicts/issues, 14
Oedipal stages (see phallic), 106
Oral stage, 105
Outpatient
 family treatment, 16
 practice, 33
 treatment, 124
  plans, 25
  staff, 25

Pathological homeostasis, 114
Patient-centered treatment, 14
Patient-therapist relationship, 104
Peer modeling, 62
Phallic stage (see oedipal), 106
Philadelphia Child Guidance
 Clinic, 95, 99
Problem/conflict resolution
 skills, 55
Problem solving, 54-55
Process
 feeling, 30
 intellectual, 30
Professional biases, 26
Psychiatric evaluation, 14
Psychiatric setting, 5, 121
 problems of, 26
 staff, 18
Psychiatry, 34
Psychoanalytic framework, 32
 and psychodynamic, 102